WILLIAMS
SONOMA
CALIFORNIA

Rustic Mexican

Authentic flavors for everyday cooking

DEBORAH SCHNEIDER

photography
JOHN LEE

weldon**owen**

contents

As a young woman, I traveled extensively before settling in Southern California, where I found myself cooking in kitchens where all of my co-workers were from Mexico. As we worked on the line, we would talk about where we were from and, of course, about food, because that's what cooks talk about. The way to our hearts is definitely through our stomachs. This is how I fell in love with the romantic story that is Mexican cuisine.

My co-workers shared wonderful memories about growing up in tiny *pueblos*, and spoke with nostalgic longing of the food that their mothers and grandmothers cooked. They told stories about foraging for wild greens and grasshoppers, fishing in mountain streams, turning the handle on the hand-cranked *molino* to grind the masa for the handmade tortillas that were (and still are) the heart of the Mexican table.

I grew up in a very different part of the world, far from Mexico, where snow covers the ground for a third of the year. The farm-style cooking in my little hometown was built around potatoes and beef rather than chiles and corn. Still, as rural communities do all over the world, we ate food that grew or was raised locally, simply cooked, and nourishing enough to carry us through days of hard work in a tough climate. I confess that I still prefer this kind of honest simplicity to the most elaborate and refined haute cuisine.

Outside Mexico, we get only the most limited taste of Mexico. Traditional Mexican cooking has a vast range, shaped by its varied regions, its history of conquest, and millennia-old indigenous foodways. Today's Mexican food is the culmination of a magnificent story, with flavors deeply rooted in that ancient countryside and not in the enormous cities, where the cooking of ranch and village has been citified and refined.

Handmade artisanship with local provenance is prized in all aspects of Mexican culture and craft, and most highly in its cooking. The handmade tortilla is the ultimate example, but even crafting a salsa or making a pot of beans is an expression of love and skill.

I like to say that most Mexican cooking can be done with a knife, a pot, a fire, and a couple of rocks, which is a bit of a stretch, but it's a fact that our true craft as cooks is found in making something beautiful with the most basic of ingredients. Mexican cooks, and the simple cooking of the Mexican countryside, prove this to be true in the most vibrant, colorful, and delicious way possible.

Schneider

small plates

Spiced nuts, sprinkled with chile and garlic, are a popular snack food wherever beer is served. This fiery trio makes the perfect foil for this refreshing beer cocktail, whose name combines the Mexican slang for "cold beer," *chelada*, and the given name of the bartender, Michel Esper, who is said to have created it at the Club Deportivo Portofino in San Luis Potosí.

spicy nuts & seeds with michelada cocktail

FOR THE NUTS & SEEDS

1 tablespoon peanut oil

10 small cloves garlic

1½ cups (220 g) raw peanuts, skins rubbed off

1½ cups (240 g) raw pumpkin seeds

1 cup (125 g) pecan halves

Fine sea salt

About 1 teaspoon ground dried árbol chile or cayenne

makes 4 cups (1¼ lb/625 g)

FOR EACH MICHELADA

1 lime wedge

Kosher salt, sea salt, or smoked salt, for rim of glass

Chile powder, for rim of glass (optional)

1 tablespoon fresh lime juice

¼ teaspoon *each* hot sauce and Worcestershire sauce

Cracked ice, for serving

1 bottle Mexican lager, such as Tecate

1 pickled jalapeño (optional)

makes 1 cocktail

To prepare the nuts and seeds, preheat the oven to 275°F (140°C). In a frying pan, heat the oil over medium-low heat. Add the garlic and sauté until they begin to turn tan, 3–4 minutes. Stir in the nuts and seeds, coating them well with the oil. Add about 1 teaspoon salt and the ground chile, just a pinch at a time, until the taste just tingles the tongue.

Transfer the nuts and seeds to a baking sheet, spreading them evenly. Bake for 15–20 minutes, stirring occasionally.

Meanwhile, to prepare each Michelada, rub the rim of a tall glass with the lime wedge. Dip the rim of the glass into a small saucer of salt, mixed with chile powder, if desired. Add lime juice, Worcestershire, and hot sauce to the glass, and then add cracked ice to half-fill the glass.

Pour in beer just shy of the salt rim and stir to combine. Garnish with a pickled jalapeño, if you like.

When the nuts are ready, the air will be filled with their rich aroma. Transfer the nuts to a bowl, sprinkle with more salt if needed, and serve warm or at room temperature.

COOK'S NOTE: To make Micheladas for a party, multiply and mix all the ingredients, except for the ice and beer, in a pitcher. As guests arrive, pour shots of the mix into tall glasses and fill with ice and beer.

This variation of *sopes* is made with fresh corn masa mixed with whole black beans, patted out thick, toasted, and topped with flavorful refried beans, tart *salsa verde*, lots of aged Mexican añejo cheese, and a fresh salsa. The speckled appearance of the corn masa bases gives them their name, which refers to the pony, rather than the bean.

"pintos"

Fine sea salt

1¾ cups (425 ml) warm water

2 tablespoons fresh pork lard or vegetable oil, plus more for greasing and brushing

2 cups (8 oz/230 g) masa harina

1½ cups (270 g) cooked black beans, rinsed (one 15-oz/425-g can)

½ small serrano chile, minced (optional)

6 sprigs fresh cilantro, chopped

1 cup (180 g) refried black beans, preferably homemade (page 115 or 172), heated

1½ cups (350 ml) *salsa verde,* preferably homemade (page 145)

1 cup (4 oz/100 g) grated queso añejo or Romano cheese

1 cup (9 oz/250 g) *pico de gallo* salsa, preferably homemade (page 129)

Diced white onion, for serving (optional)

makes 16 *sopes*

Dissolve 1½ teaspoons salt in the warm water and add the lard. Put the masa harina in a bowl. Add the salted water all at once and mix with one hand to form a smooth dough. Add the black beans, serrano (if using), and cilantro and work the dough for a minute to break up the beans a little. Cover loosely.

Heat a heavy frying pan over medium heat. Lightly grease the pan and have a brush handy. Form the masa into ¼-cup balls, then pat the balls into disks 3 inches (7.5 cm) in diameter and about ⅜ inch (1 cm) thick. Brush lightly with oil and toast on both sides until lightly golden. When the masa feels springy to the touch, remove the *pintos* from the pan, let cool slightly, and quickly pinch around the top edges to form a shallow lip (or use a small pair of tongs to pinch if this is too hot for your fingertips). Stack the *pintos* and wrap the stack in aluminum foil to keep warm to serve immediately, or refrigerate until ready to serve and reheat in a dry pan until crisp.

Top each *pinto* with warmed refried beans, *salsa verde,* a good pinch of grated cheese, a dollop of *pico de gallo,* and onions, if desired.

COOK'S NOTE: The *sope* lends itself to many variations; I also love it with carnitas and crunchy *chicharrones* piled on top. Vegetarians can substitute vegetable oil for lard and top the *pintos* with diced cooked nopales, mushrooms, and/or other salsas. Flavor the masa with chopped chipotles or anything else that takes your fancy.

Cactus of many types plays an important role in central Mexican cooking. The de-spined and boiled paddles of *opuntia* (beavertail) cactus are most commonly eaten, with a taste and texture similar to that of a cooked green bean. This *antojito*, or snack, is a miniature version of a popular street food.

nopales roasted with cheese & salsa

12 small nopal cactus paddles, about 3 inches (7.5 cm) long, or 4 large paddles, spines removed if possible

Fine sea salt

1 serrano chile

½ cup (4½ oz/125 g) *pico de gallo* salsa, preferably homemade (page 129)

1 tablespoon extra-virgin olive oil

2 cups (8 oz/225 g) shredded Menonita, Oaxaca, or Monterey Jack cheese

⅓ cup (1½ oz/40 g) grated cotija, cotija enchilado, queso añejo, Chihuahua, or Romano cheese

12 thin slices pickled jalapeño chile

serves 4–6

If your cactus still has its spines, turn on a gas burner or gas grill. Holding each paddle with a pair of metal tongs, pass it quickly through the flame to singe the small spines. Set on a towel to cool. (If a gas flame is unavailable, omit this step.) Then, holding with tongs again, use the blunt back edge of a knife to scrape away all spines. Trim the edges. If using larger nopales, cut into 2-inch (5-cm) square pieces.

Bring 2 quarts water and 1 tablespoon salt to a boil. Add the nopales and cook until olive green and al dente, about 5 minutes. Drain and rinse well under cold water, then pat dry.

Meanwhile, mince the serrano and stir it into the *pico de gallo*.

Position an oven rack 4–6 inches (10–15 cm) below the broiler and preheat on high. Place the nopales on a lightly oiled baking sheet. Drizzle with the olive oil and divide the grated cheese among them, piling it into little mounds on each. Broil the nopales until the cheese is lightly browned. Top each with a teaspoon of *pico de gallo* and a slice of pickled jalapeño. Serve hot.

COOK'S NOTE: Another method of preparing the nopal is to singe or scrape off the needles with a knife, blanch the paddles in boiling water for 3 minutes, then grill on both sides before cutting into pieces.

These Oaxacan-style breakfast quesadillas are oversized, almost like empanadas. Among the fillings you'll find *tinga* (page 86); a mix of squash blossoms, epazote, and Oaxacan cheese; the corn fungus *huitlacoche;* or this garlicky filling of mushrooms.

mushroom quesadillas

FOR THE MUSHROOMS

2 tablespoons unsalted butter or safflower oil

1 white onion, finely chopped

1 serrano chile, finely chopped

6 cloves garlic, minced

12 oz (350 g) fresh mushrooms, preferably portobello, porcini, or other flavorful variety, brushed clean and coarsely chopped

2 tablespoons minced fresh epazote leaves (optional)

Fine sea salt and freshly ground black pepper

FOR THE QUESADILLAS

1 lb (450 g) freshly prepared tortilla masa or 1¾ cups (7 oz/200 g) masa harina for tortillas

Fine sea salt

Warm water

1½ cups (6 oz/170 g) shredded quesillo de Oaxaca, Muenster, or mozzarella cheese (optional)

1 cup (250 ml) *salsa verde,* preferably homemade (page 145)

serves 4–6

To prepare the mushrooms, in a frying pan, melt the butter or heat the oil over high heat. Add the onion and chile and sauté until the onion is translucent, about 30 seconds. Add the garlic and sauté for a few seconds. Toss in the mushrooms and cook for about 4 minutes, tossing every minute or so. When the mushrooms just begin to give off their liquid, stir in the epazote (if using), ½ teaspoon salt, and ½ teaspoon pepper and remove from the heat. Let cool.

To make the quesadillas, if using fresh masa, put it in a bowl and knead with 1 teaspoon salt, adding a little warm water, if needed, to make a soft dough. If using masa harina, put in a bowl, add 1¼ cups (300 ml) plus 2 tablespoons warm water, and mix with your hands; let the dough rest for 5 minutes, then add 1 teaspoon salt and knead for 1 minute. Shape the dough into balls 1½ inches (4 cm) in diameter and cover with a damp kitchen towel or plastic wrap. Use a tortilla press lined with plastic wrap to flatten the balls into thin disks (see page 178), pressing hard so that they will be about 6–7 inches (15–18 cm) in diameter. Rotate the dough on the plastic and press again so that all sides are of equal thickness.

Remove the top piece of plastic and place 1 tablespoon of the shredded cheese, if using, in the center of the lower half of each tortilla, keeping the edge free. Spoon on some mushrooms. Fold the other half of the tortilla over the filling and press the edges together with your fingers. Lift up the bottom piece of plastic and turn the quesadilla over to remove it. Repeat until all quesadillas are made.

Heat a *comal,* griddle, or large, heavy frying pan over medium-high heat. When hot, gently lay one quesadilla on the hot surface and cook until it starts to brown, 1 minute. Turn the quesadilla and move it to the side to continue cooking, while starting the next one. Repeat the process, and when the quesadillas are well cooked and browned on each side, carefully remove to a 200°F oven to keep warm.

Serve the quesadillas at once, if possible, with the salsa on the side.

The secret to making these long rolled tacos is the *raspadas*, tortillas that have had the top layer literally rasped off and discarded, before they are wrapped around a tasty filling and fried until crisp. If time is a concern, omit this step and simply use regular corn tortillas.

shredded chicken flautas

FOR THE FILLING

2 bone-in chicken breasts

¼ white onion plus ½ cup (60 g) chopped white onion

1 tablespoon safflower or canola oil

3 serrano chiles, seeded and chopped

1 clove garlic, minced

1 large, ripe tomato, finely chopped, or half a 14.5-oz (400-g) can diced tomatoes, drained

Fine sea salt

12 thin corn tortillas, 6–7 inches (15–18 cm) in diameter

Canola oil for frying

FOR SERVING

2 cups (6 oz/180 g) thinly shredded cabbage, seasoned with the juice of 1 lime (optional)

Avocado salsa, preferably homemade (page 142)

1 cup (250 ml) *crema*, preferably homemade (page 177), or sour cream

12 radishes, sliced (optional)

Pasilla and Árbol Chile Salsa (page 142)

serves 6

To make the filling, put the chicken in a large saucepan and add 1 qt (1 L) water and the ¼ onion. Bring to a boil, reduce the heat to medium, cover, and simmer until the chicken is cooked through, 15–20 minutes. Remove the chicken and set aside to cool, reserving the stock for another use. Shred the meat, discarding the skin and bones.

In a frying pan, heat the oil over medium heat. Add the chopped onion, chiles, and garlic and sauté just until softened, about 3 minutes. Raise the heat to medium-high, add the tomato, and cook, stirring occasionally, until the excess moisture is absorbed, 10–15 minutes longer. Remove from the heat and stir in the shredded chicken and salt to taste. Set aside.

If making the *raspadas,* heat a dry heavy frying pan over low heat. Place a tortilla on it and allow it to just dry out without browning, 3–5 minutes. Remove from the pan and immediately use a table knife to scrape and then pull off the top layer of the tortilla, which should puff up, making it easier to scrape. Repeat to rasp off the tops of the remaining tortillas.

To fry the tortillas, pour about 3 tablespoons oil into a deep, heavy frying pan and heat over medium-high heat. When the oil is hot but not smoking, pass each tortilla briefly through it, turning once. Transfer to paper towels.

To form each flauta, put a large spoonful of the filling along the center of a tortilla, roll up tightly, and secure with a wooden toothpick, if necessary.

Add oil to a depth of 1 inch (2.5 cm) into the same frying pan and place over medium-high heat until hot. Working in batches, add the flautas to the oil and fry, turning several times to cook evenly, until lightly browned and crisp, about 2 minutes. Using tongs, lift the flautas out of the oil, allowing any excess oil to run off, and lean them against a pan on absorbent paper so they can completely drain. Keep warm in a 200°F oven while frying the rest of the flautas.

Line a serving platter with the cabbage, if using, then top with the flautas. Drizzle with the avocado salsa and *crema*. Garnish with the radishes, if using, and serve the chile salsa on the side. Serve right away.

Using classic *pibil* flavors of achiote and sour orange on grilled pork ribs is a delicious spin on tradition. A quick turn in a savory salsa keeps the pork juicy and succulent. The same marinade is excellent on grilled meaty fish.

grilled pork ribs

4 lb (2 kg) meaty pork back ribs

Fine sea salt

2 tablespoons achiote paste (page 182)

½ cup (125 ml) fresh bitter orange juice (page 185)

4 cloves garlic, minced

2 large, ripe tomatoes

¼ white onion

1 habanero chile

¼ cup (15 g) coarsely chopped fresh cilantro

serves 8

Cut the ribs into sections of 4 or 5 ribs each and place in a large pot. Add water to cover and 1 or 2 teaspoons salt. Bring to a boil, skimming off any foam from the surface. Reduce the heat to low, cover, and simmer until nearly cooked, about 35 minutes. Transfer the ribs to a glass bowl. In a bowl, dissolve the achiote paste in the orange juice. Stir in the garlic and a good amount of salt. Pour over the ribs, mix well, cover, and refrigerate for at least 6 hours or up to 24 hours.

Prepare an indirect-heat fire in a charcoal grill. Meanwhile, roast the tomatoes, onion, and chile (see page 178). Remove the ribs from the marinade, place on the grill rack, and grill, turning often, until crispy brown, about 15 minutes.

Combine the tomatoes, onion, and chile in a blender or food processor and blend until smooth. Pour the purée into a saucepan and heat to serving temperature.

Remove the ribs from the grill and cut into one-rib portions. Add the ribs to the sauce and simmer, uncovered, over low heat, for 10 minutes. Taste and adjust the seasoning.

Arrange the ribs on a platter, spoon the sauce over them, and sprinkle with the cilantro. Serve at once.

A classic steak tartare is given a spicy Mexican edge with the addition of serrano chiles, cilantro, and fresh lime juice—rather like a raw beef ceviche. Such combinations of raw meat with typical Mexican flavors are a common *botana* (snack) in the north of the country.

carne apache

1¼ lb (600 g) filet mignon, trimmed of excess fat and sinew (see Cook's Note)

1 baguette, thinly sliced on the diagonal

2 teaspoons olive oil, plus more for brushing

Fine sea salt and freshly ground black pepper

⅓ cup (50 g) finely chopped red onion

⅓ cup (50 g) capers, rinsed and finely chopped

3 serrano chiles, seeded and very finely chopped

1½ tablespoons minced fresh cilantro

1 tablespoon Worcestershire sauce

1½ teaspoons Dijon mustard

Dash of hot-pepper sauce, such as Tabasco

4 small egg yolks (see Cook's Note)

4 limes, quartered

Coarse sea salt, for serving

serves 4

Place the beef on a baking sheet and freeze, uncovered, for 20 minutes. Place a bowl and four plates in the freezer to chill.

Preheat the oven to 350°F (180°C). Brush the baguette slices lightly with olive oil and season with salt and pepper. Spread in a single layer on a baking sheet and toast until golden brown, about 10 minutes.

Cut the beef across the grain into thin slices. Stack the slices, a few at a time, and cut into thin strips. Stack a few strips and cut crosswise into a fine dice. In the very cold bowl, stir together the onion, capers, chiles, cilantro, Worcestershire sauce, mustard, 2 teaspoons olive oil, and a dash of hot-pepper sauce. Add the beef and mix with a fork to distribute the ingredients evenly; avoid compacting the beef.

Divide the mixture among the very cold plates. With the back of a spoon, make a well in the center of each serving. Gently deposit an egg yolk in each well. (Alternatively, leave each yolk in half of the shell and nestle in the meat; diners pour the yolk onto the meat and mix to incorporate.) Garnish with the lime wedges. Serve at once with the toasted baguette slices and with salt on the side for seasoning.

COOK'S NOTE: If you choose to prepare beef raw, be sure to buy high-quality meat from a reputable butcher. Eating raw beef entails some degree of risk of bacterial contamination, including E. coli. The latter can make a healthy adult ill; the risk is greater for the very young, the elderly, pregnant women, or anyone with a compromised immune system. Eating raw eggs also carries some risk due to the threat of salmonella bacteria, though the incidence of contamination is extremely low. However, to be safe, the same people who should avoid raw beef should avoid raw eggs.

If there is a dish that cries out for homemade tortillas, this is it. If possible, use freshly ground masa from a local tortilla factory or other source—there is nothing like it. Masa can also be made from packaged masa harina, which is ground dried masa, but it will not have the same body or flavor as the freshly made dough.

quesadillas with poblano chiles

FOR THE TORTILLAS

19 oz (540 g) freshly prepared tortilla masa or 2 cups (8 oz/230 g) masa harina for tortillas

Fine sea salt

Warm water

FOR THE FILLING

1 tablespoon safflower or canola oil, plus more for frying

1 white onion, thinly sliced

2 cloves garlic, minced

½ teaspoon dried oregano, preferably Mexican

2 poblano chiles, roasted, peeled, and seeded (page 178), then cut lengthwise into 12 strips, each ¼ inch (6 mm) wide

8 oz (250 g) quesillo de Oaxaca, Muenster, or Monterey Jack cheese, shredded (about 2 cups)

12 fresh epazote leaves (optional)

Guacamole (page 126) and Salsa Fresca (page 129) or Salsa Verde (page 145), for serving

serves 6

To make the tortillas, if using fresh masa, put it in a bowl and knead with 1 teaspoon salt, adding a little warm water, if needed, to make a soft dough. If using masa harina, put in a bowl, add 1¼ cups (300 ml) plus 2 tablespoons warm water, and mix with your hands; let the dough rest for 5 minutes, then add 1 teaspoon salt and knead for 1 minute. Shape the dough into 12 golf ball–sized balls, then cover with a damp kitchen towel or plastic wrap.

To make the filling, in a frying pan, heat the oil over medium heat. Add the onion and sauté until golden brown, about 5 minutes. Stir in the garlic and oregano and continue cooking for 1 minute. Add the poblanos and ½ teaspoon salt and toss until everything is thoroughly heated. Taste and adjust the seasoning.

To make the quesadillas, use a tortilla press lined with plastic wrap to flatten the masa into thin disks (see page 178). Remove the top piece of plastic and place a generous tablespoon of the shredded cheese on half of the tortilla, keeping the edge free. Top with 1 epazote leaf, if using, and a chile strip with a few onion slices. Lift the lower piece of plastic to fold the uncovered side of the tortilla over the filling.

Press the edges together with your fingers, remove from the press, and set aside, covered with a barely damp towel. Repeat until all the quesadillas are made.

Preheat the oven to 200°F (90°C). In a deep, heavy frying pan, heat 1 inch (2.5 cm) oil over medium-high heat until the oil shimmers. Fry the quesadillas, one at a time, until golden, 1–2 minutes. Using a slotted spatula, transfer to paper towels. Let drain briefly, then transfer to a heatproof platter and keep warm in the oven. When all the quesadillas are cooked, serve at once with the guacamole and salsa.

COOK'S NOTE: Quick quesadillas may be made with thin, purchased white-corn tortillas, but they will not seal as well—or taste as good—as homemade tortillas.

The much-loved flavor of carnitas, or "little meats," is derived from pork that has been slow-cooked until meltingly tender. As the liquid evaporates during cooking, the meat browns in its own fat, creating succulent yet crispy bits of meat.

carnitas tacos

3 lb (1.5 kg) boneless pork shoulder or country-style ribs

6 cloves garlic, halved

Zest of 1 orange, cut into strips

¾ cup (180 ml) fresh orange juice

Fine sea salt

1 tablespoon canola or safflower oil, if needed

FOR SERVING

12 corn tortillas, preferably homemade (page 106), warmed

Lime wedges

Roughly torn fresh cilantro leaves

Pickled Red Onions (page 139)

Salsa fresca, preferably homemade (page 129)

serves 6

Cut off any big pieces of fat from the pork and put the fat in a heavy saucepan or frying pan wide enough to accommodate the pork in a single layer. Cut the pork into strips about 1½ inches (4 cm) long and ¾ inch (2 cm) wide. Add the pork to the pan with the garlic, orange zest, orange juice, and 2 teaspoons salt. Add water to barely cover the meat and bring to a boil over medium heat. Reduce the heat to medium low, cover partially, and cook, stirring occasionally, until all of the liquid has evaporated, about 1 hour. If the meat is not yet fork tender, add a bit more water and continue cooking.

Uncover the pan and continue cooking the pork until all the fat is rendered and the meat is browning in the melted fat, 10–15 minutes longer. There is usually enough melted fat in the pan, but if the pan seems dry and lacking in fat, add the 1 tablespoon oil.

When the meat is browned and crisp, using a slotted spoon, transfer it to a colander and let any excess fat drain away. Transfer the meat to a serving bowl. Place the tortillas on a plate and place the lime wedges, cilantro, pickled onions, and salsa in individual bowls. Allow diners to assemble their own tacos as they desire.

COOK'S NOTE: Instead of as tacos, you can serve the carnitas on individual plates with refried beans (page 172), steamed rice, and salsa. Or, serve as part of Fideos Norteños (page 62).

Light and satisfying ceviches are typical of coastal Mexican cuisine. In the Veracruz style, fresh lime juice firms up delicate seafood while olives add brininess to balance out sweet tomatoes and a kick of heat from the serrano chile. Use sashimi-grade firm, white-fleshed fish such as sea bass, rock cod, sole, halibut, or flounder.

halibut ceviche with avocado

1¼ lb (600 g) halibut fillets, or other white fish fillets

½ cup (125 ml) fresh lime juice

2 firm but ripe tomatoes, peeled, seeded, and cut into small dice

2–3 serrano chiles, seeded and minced

⅓ cup (20 g) chopped fresh cilantro

Fine sea salt and freshly ground black pepper

1 avocado

10 green olives, preferably Manzanillas, pitted and coarsely chopped

1 teaspoon dried oregano, preferably Mexican

2 tablespoons extra-virgin olive oil

Fried tortilla chips or strips, preferably homemade (Totopos, page 107)

serves 6

Cut the fish fillets into ½-inch (12-mm) cubes and put them into a large glass or ceramic bowl. Pour the lime juice over the fish, making sure all the pieces are covered. Let the fish stand in the lime juice until opaque and firm, 2–3 hours.

Drain and pat the fish dry with paper towels. Put the fish cubes back into the bowl and add the tomatoes, chiles, cilantro, and salt and pepper to taste. Stir to mix well and refrigerate for at least 2 hours.

When ready to serve, pit, peel, and dice the avocado and stir it into the fish mixture, along with the olives and oregano. Drizzle the ceviche with the olive oil and spoon into 6 individual serving glasses. Serve right away with *totopos,* or chill before serving for up to 12 hours.

Beautiful yellow squash blossoms *(flor de calabasa)* are delicious with a filling of corn, fresh chiles, and queso fresco, a mildly salty fresh cheese. Epazote, a native herb with a taste somewhere between mint and marjoram, is a distinctive addition to many traditional Mexican recipes.

stuffed squash blossoms

1 ear sweet white corn, husks and silks removed

2 tablespoons olive oil

½ white or red onion, finely diced

1 large clove garlic, minced

½ serrano chile, stemmed, seeded, and minced (optional)

1 cup (5 oz/150 g) finely diced zucchini

1 plum tomato, seeded and finely diced

Fine sea salt and freshly ground black pepper

1 tablespoon minced fresh epazote leaves

12 large squash blossoms

4 oz (100 g) queso fresco or goat cheese, cut into ½-inch (12-mm) cubes

2 tablespoons crumbled cotija or feta cheese (optional)

Fire-Roasted Tomato Salsa (page 144), for serving

serves 4–6

Hold the shucked ear of corn upright on a cutting board or in a small bowl and, using a sharp knife, cut off the kernels, keeping the blade angled inward so you get the whole kernel but none of the tough cob. You should have about ¾ cup (130 g) kernels. Set aside.

In a frying pan, heat 1 tablespoon of the olive oil over medium-high heat. Add the onion, garlic, and chile (if using) and cook, stirring constantly, until fragrant, about 1 minute. Add the corn, zucchini, and tomato and cook, stirring constantly, until the vegetables are tender-crisp, 2–3 minutes longer. Season with ½ teaspoon salt and ¼ teaspoon pepper. Remove from the heat and stir in the epazote. Taste and adjust the seasoning. Set the filling aside.

To clean the squash blossoms, have ready a bowl of cold, lightly salted water. Remove the small green leaves beneath the flower. If there is a stem, leave it on; the pistils and stamens may be left in or removed. Swish the blossoms quickly in the salt water and hold upside down to drain briefly, then place on paper towels to drain further. Pat gently with paper towels to dry completely before stuffing.

Carefully tear a slit down 1 side of each squash blossom. Tuck 2 or 3 cubes of the queso fresco into the bottom of each blossom. Using a small spoon, stuff each blossom with about 1 tablespoon of the vegetable filling, or as much as it can hold without tearing or spilling out. Overlap the petals to close the opening and press gently to compact the filling.

In a large frying pan, heat the remaining olive oil over medium heat. Working in batches, add the stuffed squash blossoms and cook gently until light golden brown and heated through, about 4 minutes, turning once. The queso will soften but not melt. Transfer to individual plates or a platter, sprinkle with the cotija (if using), and a dollop of tomato salsa, and serve right away.

Fresh shrimp are a staple of coastal Oaxacan cooking. Adding sweet shrimp to a fresh, lively *pico de gallo* creates a substantial and delicious *botana* (appetizer) that's great with chips, rolled in tortillas, or used as an accompaniment to grilled fish or vegetables.

pico de gallo with shrimp

2 lb (1 kg) plum tomatoes, roughly chopped

8 oz (250 g) cooked small shrimp, peeled and roughly chopped

½ cup (120 g) roughly chopped pickled jalapeño chiles, plus ¼ cup (50 ml) brine from jar

½ cup (30 g) roughly chopped fresh cilantro

1 small white onion, roughly chopped

Juice of 3 limes

Fine sea salt

serves 6–8

In a large bowl, combine the tomatoes, shrimp, jalapeños plus brine, cilantro, onion, and lime juice. Season with salt to taste and let sit at room temperature for at least 1 hour to blend the flavors before serving.

COOK'S NOTE: A sturdy salsa like this is great with chips, but even better served over grilled vegetables or white fish or simply wrapped in tortillas as a snack.

A freshly fried, crisp tostada stacked high with a savory topping is a popular street food everywhere in Mexico. This version layers spicy beans and plump shrimp with guacamole, and gets its zip from a fiery tomato salsa. Make a half-size version for parties, or substitute chicken or grilled steak for the shrimp.

shrimp tostadas

FOR THE SPICY PINTOS

1 tablespoon lard or oil

½ white onion, finely chopped

½ tomato, peeled, seeded, and diced

2 cloves garlic, minced

1 jalapeño chile, thinly sliced into rings

Fine sea salt and freshly ground black pepper

1½ cups (270 g) cooked pinto beans, rinsed (one 15-oz/425-g can)

1 tablespoon chopped fresh cilantro

Safflower or canola oil for frying

8 corn tortillas, 5 inches (13 cm) in diameter

24 medium shrimp, peeled and deveined

1 tablespoon chili powder

2 teaspoons ground cumin

Guacamole (page 126), for topping

½ cup (2 oz/60 g) crumbled queso fresco or goat cheese

Fire-Roasted Tomato Salsa (page 144), for serving

¼ cup (7 g) loosely packed fresh cilantro leaves

serves 4

To make the beans, in a sauté pan, melt the lard or heat the oil over medium heat. Add the onion and cook, stirring often, until translucent, about 5 minutes. Add the tomato, garlic, jalapeño, ½ teaspoon salt, and ½ teaspoon black pepper and cook until the tomato is tender and begins to break down, about 10 minutes. Add the beans and cook, stirring occasionally, until almost all of the liquid is absorbed and the mixture has the consistency of a thick sauce, about 10 minutes longer. Cover to keep warm until ready to serve.

To make the tostadas, in a small, heavy frying pan, heat 1 inch (2.5 cm) oil over medium-high heat to 375°F (190°C) on a deep-frying thermometer. (If you don't have a thermometer, dip the edge of a tortilla into the oil; it should sizzle immediately and vigorously.)

Line a plate with paper towels. Using tongs, add the tortillas one at a time to the hot oil and fry, lifting out as soon as their color deepens. Drain on the paper towels. Sprinkle with salt while the tortillas are still warm.

Heat a grill pan or a cast-iron frying pan over high heat. In a bowl, toss the shrimp with 1 tablespoon oil, the chili powder, and cumin. Season with salt and add to the hot pan. Grill or sear, turning once, until the shrimp are bright pink and opaque throughout, about 2 minutes per side. Transfer to a plate and set aside.

To assemble the tostadas, put two tortillas on each of four individual plates and layer on the toppings in this order: guacamole, pinto beans, shrimp, queso fresco, and salsa. Garnish with the cilantro leaves and serve right away.

Even a badly dented plow disk is not discarded by farmers in northern Mexico. Instead, it is used over a wood fire for cooking this robust, easygoing dish. If you haven't got a battered old disk handy, I suggest substituting the similarly shaped wok. Serve the burritos with refried beans (page 172).

farmer's-style burritos

2 white onions, finely chopped, plus ½ onion for rubbing

8 oz (250 g) lean bacon, chopped

8 oz (250 g) Mexican chorizo, casings removed and sausage crumbled

1 red bell pepper, seeded and chopped

3 ripe tomatoes, roasted (page 178) and chopped, or 1 can (14.5 oz/400 g) diced tomatoes, partially drained

12 oz (350 g) pork tenderloin or boneless country-style ribs, cut into ¾-inch (2-cm) chunks

1 lb (500 g) beef sirloin tip, cut into ¾-inch (2-cm) chunks

1 serrano chile, finely chopped

Fine sea salt

¼ head lettuce, finely shredded

1 cup (8 oz/250 g) guacamole, preferably homemade (page 126) (optional)

Salsa of choice

8–10 flour tortillas, 8 inches (20 cm) in diameter

serves 8

Heat a wok over medium-high heat and rub the chunk of onion around the pan several times to season it; discard the onion. Add the bacon, and when the fat starts to melt, stir in the chorizo and fry, stirring constantly, until the meats are cooked but not starting to brown or crisp, 8–10 minutes.

Add the chopped onions and bell pepper to the wok, reduce the heat to medium-low, and fry until the onions are golden, about 10 minutes. Spoon the excess fat into a large frying pan. Add the tomatoes to the wok and continue to cook for several minutes until the tomatoes are very soft and some liquid remains.

Meanwhile, heat the bacon and chorizo fat in the frying pan over medium-high heat. Add the pork and beef and cook until any liquid evaporates and the meat begins to caramelize, about 5 minutes. Add the meat to the wok and stir to mix well. Add the chile, season with salt to taste, and heat through.

Set out the lettuce, guacamole, and salsa. Place a *comal*, griddle, or heavy frying pan over medium-high heat. Place a tortilla on the hot surface and heat briefly, turning once. Transfer to a plate and top with some of the meat. Spoon some of the condiments on top, loosely fold the tortilla over the meat, and serve. Alternatively, fold the bottom of the tortilla over the filling, fold in the two sides, left and then right, and finish by rolling up the tortilla until it is completely closed, then eat out of hand.

Basically a refried-bean sandwich, *molletes* are a favorite breakfast on the go, but you can snack on them all day (and night) from street stands or even small markets. If you can't get a real Mexican *bolillo* roll, a French roll, Kaiser roll, or a baguette will do. I like to add lots of pickled jalapeños and onions to mine.

grilled bean & cheese sandwiches

FOR THE SALSA

2 lb (1 kg) plum tomatoes, diced

⅔ cup (40 g) roughly chopped fresh cilantro

6 serrano or 4 jalapeño chiles, seeded and finely chopped

1 large white onion, finely chopped

Fine sea salt and freshly ground black pepper

FOR THE REFRIED BEANS

½ cup (125 ml) safflower or canola oil

4 cloves garlic, minced

1 small white onion, finely chopped

2 cups (500 ml) chicken stock, preferably homemade (page 173)

4½ cups (810 g) cooked pinto beans, rinsed (three 15-oz/425-g cans)

Fine sea salt and freshly ground black pepper

4 *bolillos* or Kaiser rolls

12 oz (340 g) Chihuahua or Monterey Jack cheese, grated

serves 8

To make the salsa, in a bowl, combine the tomatoes, cilantro, chiles, and onion and season liberally with salt and pepper; fold gently to combine. Cover and refrigerate to blend flavors, about 1 hour.

To prepare the refried beans, heat the oil in a 12-inch (30-cm) frying pan over medium-high heat. Add the garlic and onion and cook, stirring, until soft, about 8 minutes. Add the stock and beans and cook, stirring and mashing, until almost all the beans are smooth and the mixture is slightly soupy, about 5 minutes. Season with salt and pepper and keep warm.

Heat the broiler to high. Split each roll horizontally and scoop out the insides from the tops and bottoms, leaving a shell about ½ inch (12 mm) thick; discard the insides. Place the roll halves on a foil-lined baking sheet with cut sides up and broil until lightly toasted, about 2 minutes. Pour about ½ cup (120 g) refried beans over each roll half so that the beans are spilling over the edges, then sprinkle with cheese. Return to the broiler and heat until the beans are heated through and the cheese is just melted, but not browned, about 2 minutes.

Transfer one roll half to each serving plate and top each with a couple large spoonfuls of salsa. Serve immediately.

COOK'S NOTE: In a pinch, canned refried beans and store-bought *pico de gallo* can be used to make this quick and satisfying dish.

Spice-crusted salmon gets crisp on the outside and stays moist and tender on the inside when seared in a hot pan. You can also serve the flaked salmon, spicy cabbage, and salsa atop a bed of Seasoned White Rice (page 177).

blackened salmon tacos

2 tablespoons all-purpose flour

1½ tablespoons chili powder

1 tablespoon dark brown sugar

1 teaspoon onion powder

1 teaspoon garlic powder

1 teaspoon smoked paprika

Fine sea salt and freshly ground black pepper

2 lb (1 kg) center-cut salmon fillet, pin bones and skin removed

2 tablespoons olive oil

FOR THE SPICY CABBAGE

2 tablespoons sherry vinegar

½ teaspoon Dijon mustard

1 tablespoon olive oil

¼ small green cabbage or Savoy cabbage, shredded (about 2 cups/180 g)

8–12 flour or corn tortillas, preferably homemade (page 106), warmed

Pineapple-Jicama Salsa (page 134), for serving

serves 4–6

In a small bowl, stir together the flour, chili powder, brown sugar, onion powder, garlic powder, smoked paprika, and ¼ teaspoon salt. Pat the salmon dry with a paper towel, then coat on all sides with the spice rub.

In a nonstick frying pan, heat the olive oil over high heat. Add the salmon to the hot oil and cook, turning once, for about 5 minutes per side for rare. To get a nice sear, be sure not to move the salmon in the pan for the 5 minutes. Transfer to a cutting board, cover loosely with aluminum foil, and let rest for about 10 minutes.

Meanwhile, make the spicy cabbage: In the bottom of a large bowl, stir together the vinegar and mustard and season with salt and pepper. Whisk in the olive oil until well blended. Add the cabbage and toss to coat thoroughly with the dressing. Taste and adjust the seasoning.

Transfer the salmon to a platter and, using a fork, flake the salmon into large chunks. To serve, set out the platter of salmon along with the tortillas, salsa, and cabbage and let diners create their own tacos.

All over Mexico, bowls of these brightly colored, lightly pickled vegetables—a perfect condiment to serve with *antojitos*, or snacks—are set out on the counters of little market restaurants called *fondas*. I especially like this chunky Oaxacan version.

pickled mixed vegetables

4 whole heads garlic

½ cup (125 ml) safflower or canola oil

6 carrots, peeled and cut into slices ¼ inch (6 mm) thick

6 jalapeño chiles, cut into slices ½ inch (12 mm) thick

1 white onion, cut into slices ½ inch (12 mm) thick

4 cups (1 qt/1 L) mild white vinegar

2 tablespoons dried oregano, preferably Mexican

3 bay leaves

2 teaspoons peppercorns

3 whole cloves

Fine sea salt

2 cups (185 g) small cauliflower florets

20 green beans, trimmed and cut into 1½-inch (4-cm) lengths

6–8 very small potatoes, unpeeled, boiled until barely tender

makes about 2 qt (2 L)

Keeping the garlic heads whole, remove the outer layers of papery skins and slice off the tops to expose the cloves. In a large, deep frying pan, heat the oil over medium heat. Add the garlic heads and sauté, stirring often, until the skin begins to crisp, about 5 minutes. Add the carrots and cook for 2 minutes more, then stir in the chiles and onion. Continue to cook and stir for another 2 minutes. The vegetables should still be crisp.

Add the vinegar, 2 cups (500 ml) water, oregano, bay leaves, peppercorns, cloves, and about 2 teaspoons salt, and bring to a boil. Drop in the cauliflower and green beans and simmer until just tender, no more than 5 minutes. Add the potatoes and heat through.

Ladle the vegetables and liquid into 2 clean, sterilized jars (page 178) and let cool. Seal tightly and let marinate in the refrigerator overnight. Bring to room temperature before serving.

Guadalajara is famous for its *tortas ahogadas*, sandwiches filled with pork and refried beans and "drowned" in two red sauces, one mild and one spicy. These *tortas* are made with Mexico's classic roll, the *bolillo*, which is similar to a French roll, with a hard crust and a soft and flaky interior. I like mine with Pickled Red Onions (page 139).

pork sandwiches drowned with two salsas

1 rib-end pork loin, bone-in, about 3 lb (1.5 kg)

4 cloves garlic

1 teaspoon dried oregano, preferably Mexican

Fine sea salt and freshly ground black pepper

FOR THE SWEET SALSA

3 ripe tomatoes, quartered, or 1½ cups (9 oz/250 g) drained canned diced tomatoes

3 tablespoons chopped white onion

2 cloves garlic, coarsely chopped

2 pinches of ground cumin

2 pinches of dried marjoram

1 tablespoon safflower or canola oil

Preheat the oven to 350°F (180°C). Using a sharp knife, prick small holes over the surface of the meat. Smash the garlic with the oregano, 1 teaspoon salt, and ½ teaspoon pepper and massage the mixture into the pork. Put the pork in a baking dish a little larger than the piece of meat. Add water to a depth of ½ inch (12 mm). Cover with aluminum foil and roast until an instant-read thermometer inserted into the thickest part of the loin away from the bone registers 150°F (65°C), beginning to check after about 45 minutes. Remove the foil and roast until browned on top and the internal temperature reaches 155°F (68°C). Let the meat rest for 10 minutes, then coarsely chop into bite-sized pieces, discarding the bones.

Meanwhile, prepare the salsas. To make the sweet salsa, put the tomatoes, onion, garlic, cumin, marjoram, and ½ teaspoon salt in a blender or food processor. Purée until smooth. In a heavy saucepan, heat the oil over medium-high heat. Add the purée and let it bubble and sputter, stirring occasionally, until the flavors are well blended, about 5 minutes. Let cool slightly and pass through a medium-mesh sieve. This sauce can be served warm or at room temperature.

FOR THE PICANTE SALSA

3 ripe tomatoes, quartered, or 1½ cups (9 oz/250 g) drained canned diced tomatoes

15 dried árbol chiles, toasted (page 178)

¼ small white onion, chopped

2 cloves garlic, coarsely chopped

½ cup (125 ml) mild white vinegar

2 pinches of ground cumin

8 *bolillos*, Kaiser rolls, or small French rolls

2 cups (14 oz/400 g) refried pinto or other brown beans, preferably homemade (page 172), heated

2 large, ripe tomatoes, sliced

2 avocados, preferably Hass, pitted, peeled, and sliced

¼ head lettuce, shredded

2 limes, quartered

serves 8

To make the picante salsa, in a saucepan, bring the tomatoes, chiles, onion, garlic, 1 cup (250 ml) water, vinegar, cumin, and ½ teaspoon salt to a boil over medium heat, reduce the heat to low, and cook until thick and well seasoned, 20–25 minutes. Let cool slightly and pour into a blender or food processor. Process until a smooth purée forms. Pass the purée through a medium-mesh sieve. Pour into a bowl and serve at room temperature.

Slice each *bolillo* or French roll in half horizontally. Pick out some of the doughy crumbs, making a shallow nest. Spread the bottom half with the warm beans, pile on some pork, and top with tomato and avocado slices and some shredded lettuce. Since a *torta* is usually eaten out of hand, many cooks cover only half of it with the sweet salsa so it can be held with a minimum of mess, and the hotter sauce is set out in a bowl to be used very sparingly. Others cover the whole *torta* with lots of sweet salsa and just a drop or two of the liquid fire. Then there are the reckless people who drench the *torta* in the picante salsa and suffer happily. Squirt on some lime juice to accent the flavors. Serve with lots of napkins.

soups, rice & pasta

This simple, homey dish, like chilaquiles, makes use of corn tortillas left over from an earlier meal. With its layers of flavors and textures, it's the ultimate one-dish meal. The earthy tomato-chile broth thickened with a corn tortilla is a hearty, satisfying base for a variety of toppings, such as cheese, avocado, and toasted chile.

tortilla soup

6 thin corn tortillas

4 dried ancho chiles, seeded

½ cup (125 ml) safflower or canola oil, or as needed

½ white onion, chopped

2 cloves garlic, peeled but left whole

1 ripe tomato, roughly chopped, or 1⅓ cups (8 oz/250 g) drained canned diced tomatoes

6 cups (48 fl oz/1.5 L) chicken stock, preferably homemade (page 173)

4–5 fresh epazote leaves (optional)

¼ teaspoon dried oregano, preferably Mexican

Fine sea salt

½ lb (250 g) queso fresco or Monterey Jack cheese, cubed

1 avocado, pitted, peeled, and cubed

serves 6

Set one tortilla aside. Cut the other tortillas in half and then cut crosswise into strips ½ inch (12 mm) wide. Set aside. In a bowl, soak 1 chile in hot water for 10–15 minutes. Cut the other chiles lengthwise into narrow strips about 1 inch (2.5 cm) long.

In a frying pan, heat 6 tablespoons (90 ml) of the oil over medium-high heat. When hot, add the tortilla strips and fry, tossing, until crisp and golden on both sides, just a few seconds. Using a slotted spoon, transfer to paper towels to drain. Fry the chile strips very quickly in the same oil—again for just seconds—then remove and drain on paper towels.

Discard all but 1 tablespoon of the oil in the frying pan. Heat over medium-low heat, add the onion and garlic, and sauté until a rich golden brown, about 10 minutes. Transfer to a blender or food processor. Drain the soaking chile, discarding the liquid. Tear up the chile and the remaining tortilla and add to the blender or food processor with the tomato. Purée until smooth, adding up to ¼ cup (60 ml) water if needed to achieve a smooth consistency.

In a Dutch oven or other large, heavy pot, heat 1 tablespoon of the oil over medium-high heat. Add the purée and fry, stirring continuously, until the sauce has deepened in color, about 5 minutes. Stir in the stock and the epazote, if using, and simmer to blend the flavors, about 15 minutes. Add the oregano and season to taste with salt at the end of the cooking.

When ready to serve, divide half of the tortilla strips among warmed bowls, then ladle the hot soup into the bowls. Top with the remaining tortilla strips, the cheese, the chile strips, and the avocado. Serve right away.

Mexican cooks can often step outside to collect avocados growing wild in abundance. On hot summer days, this quickly prepared cold soup, pale green and with the rich but delicate flavor of the avocados, is a perfect way to start a meal.

chilled avocado soup

4 cups (1 qt/1 L) chicken stock, preferably homemade (page 173)

1 small white onion, quartered, plus 3 tablespoons chopped

3 peppercorns

4 avocados, preferably Hass

¼ cup (50 ml) fresh lime juice

1 clove garlic, minced

1 cup (250 ml) *crema,* preferably homemade (page 177), or buttermilk, plus more for garnish

1 cup (60 g) chopped fresh cilantro

½ cup (30 g) coarsely chopped fresh spinach

2 serrano chiles, chopped

Fine sea salt

Salsa Fresca (page 129), for serving

serves 6

Pour the stock into a saucepan and place over medium-high heat. Add the onion quarters and peppercorns, bring to a boil, and boil until the stock is reduced to 3 cups (700 ml), about 5 minutes. Strain, discard the solids, and let the stock cool.

Cut the avocados in half, remove the pits, and scoop out the flesh into a blender or food processor. Pour in half of the reduced chicken stock, add the lime juice, and process until smooth. Pour into a bowl and stir in the remaining stock.

Put the garlic, chopped onion, *crema,* cilantro, spinach, and chiles into the unrinsed blender and process until smooth. Stir into the avocado mixture until thoroughly blended. Taste and adjust the seasoning. Cover and refrigerate in the coldest part of the refrigerator. Chill soup bowls at the same time.

Taste the soup again and adjust the seasoning if necessary. Pour into the chilled bowls, garnish with the salsa and a dollop of *crema,* and serve.

Mushrooms of all types are widely used in traditional Mexican cooking, often paired with corn, chiles, or other staples. This full-flavored soup has a little heat from serrano chiles and a hint of epazote, a native herb with a flavor similar to mild marjoram. It is light enough to serve as a first course.

wild mushroom soup

¼ cup (50 ml) safflower or canola oil

1 white onion, finely diced

8 cloves garlic, finely diced

4 serrano chiles, seeded and finely diced

3 ripe plum tomatoes, peeled and finely diced

2 tablespoons olive oil, or as needed

2 lb (1 kg) fresh wild mushrooms, brushed clean and sliced

Fine sea salt and freshly ground black pepper

9 cups (1¼ qt/1.25 L) chicken stock, preferably homemade (page 173)

4 fresh epazote leaves, finely chopped (optional)

serves 8

In a Dutch oven or other large, heavy pot over medium-high heat, warm the safflower or canola oil. Add the onion and sauté until deep gold, about 6 minutes. Add the garlic and chiles and sauté for 1 minute longer. Stir in the tomatoes and simmer, uncovered, until very soft, about 15 minutes.

Meanwhile, in a large frying pan, heat 2 tablespoons olive oil over medium-high heat. Add the mushrooms and stir with a wooden spoon to coat evenly with the oil, adding more oil if the pan seems dry. Season with 2 teaspoons salt and some pepper and cook, stirring occasionally, until the mushrooms release their liquid, about 5 minutes.

Add the mushrooms to the onion mixture, pour in the stock, and bring to a simmer over medium-low heat. Add the epazote, if using, and stir well. Taste and adjust the seasoning, and simmer for 15–20 minutes to blend the flavors.

Ladle the soup into warmed individual bowls and serve immediately.

This dish from northern Mexico is a classic rancho soup—simple, hearty, rich with cheese, and delicious with fresh tomatoes and roasted chiles. Paired with a sprightly accompaniment like Jicama, Grapefruit, and Avocado Salad (page 113), it's a meal in itself. Some cooks like to add a little bit of beer during the final simmer.

sonoran cheese soup with potatoes

2 tablespoons unsalted butter or safflower oil

4 small new potatoes, peeled and cut into ¾-inch (2-cm) cubes

1 white onion, finely chopped

1 clove garlic, minced

2 large, ripe tomatoes, peeled and finely chopped

4 cups (1 qt/1 L) beef stock, preferably homemade (page 173)

2 California (dried Anaheim) chiles, roasted, peeled, and seeded (page 178), then chopped, or 2 canned mild green chiles, drained and chopped

1 cup (250 ml) half-and-half or whole milk, slightly warmed

Fine sea salt and freshly ground black pepper

12 oz (350 g) white Cheddar or Monterey Jack cheese, shredded (about 3 cups)

4 green onions, white and tender green parts, finely diced

serves 4–6

In a Dutch oven or other large, heavy pot, melt the butter or heat the oil over medium heat. Stir in the potatoes and onion and sauté until they begin to soften, 6–8 minutes. Do not allow to brown. Add the garlic and sauté for another minute or so.

Raise the heat to medium-high and add the tomatoes. Cook, stirring, until quite thick, about 5 minutes. Pour in the stock and chiles. Simmer, uncovered, until the potatoes are soft but not breaking apart, about 4 minutes. Reduce the heat to very low, add the half-and-half or milk, and season with salt and pepper. Cook until heated to serving temperature.

Divide the cheese evenly among warmed bowls and ladle in the soup. Garnish with the green onions and serve immediately.

Flavorful *guisados* (stews) are the heart and soul of Mexican home cooking: quick, simple, and economical one-dish meals that taste even better the next day. The *guisado* is easy to vary with any seasonal ingredients on hand—such as summer squash—or to double for a crowd.

chicken & potato stew

¼ cup (50 ml) safflower or canola oil

1½ lb (700 g) boneless, skinless chicken thighs (see Cook's Note)

Fine sea salt and freshly ground black pepper

1 small white onion, chopped

1 medium carrot, chopped

1 red bell pepper, seeded and finely chopped

1 teaspoon ground cumin

1 teaspoon dried thyme

6 cloves garlic, minced

2 canned chipotle chiles in adobo, finely chopped

1 jalapeño chile, quartered lengthwise

1 lb (500 g) Yukon Gold potatoes, peeled and cut into ½-inch (12-mm) cubes

4 cups (1 qt/1 L) chicken stock, preferably homemade (page 173)

3 sprigs fresh cilantro, plus chopped for garnish

1 can (14.5 oz/400 g) crushed tomatoes

3 tablespoons capers, rinsed

Juice of 1 lime

serves 6

Heat the oil in a 6-qt (6-L) saucepan over medium-high heat. Season the chicken with salt and pepper and, working in batches, add to pan and cook, turning once, until browned on both sides and cooked through, about 15 minutes. Transfer to a plate and let cool. When cool enough to handle, using a fork, shred the meat and set aside.

Return the saucepan to the heat and add the onion, carrot, and bell pepper and cook, stirring, until soft, about 8 minutes. Add the cumin, thyme, garlic, chipotles, and jalapeño and cook, stirring, until fragrant, about 2 minutes. Add the reserved chicken to the pan along with the potatoes, stock, cilantro, and tomatoes, and bring to a boil. Reduce the heat to medium-low and cook, stirring occasionally, until the potatoes are tender, about 30 minutes. Add the capers and lime juice and season to taste with salt and pepper before serving, garnished with chopped cilantro.

COOK'S NOTE: To make the dish even simpler to prepare, you can use leftover roast chicken (or pork) shredded into bite-sized pieces in place of the chicken thighs. Simply skip the first browning step and add the leftover meat to the stew as you would the cooked chicken thighs.

This unusual bean soup is lightened with sweet corn—more like a vegetable stew than a simple soup. A variety of spicy and savory toppings and cheeses makes the soup unique to each diner.

black bean & corn soup

2 tablespoons safflower or canola oil

1 white onion, chopped

1 clove garlic, chopped

8 cups (48 oz/1.4 kg) undrained Pot Beans (page 172) made with black beans

3 cups (700 ml) chicken stock, preferably homemade (page 173)

1 sprig fresh epazote

1 cup (180 g) corn kernels

2 scant teaspoons chicken bouillon granules

Fine sea salt and freshly ground black pepper

FOR THE CONDIMENTS

½ white onion

5 serrano chiles

3 canned chipotle chiles in adobo

1 avocado

1 cup (30 g) crumbled pork *chicharrones* (fried pork belly or rinds)

1 cup (4 oz/100 g) crumbled queso fresco or fresh goat cheese

½ cup (2 oz/60 g) grated queso añejo or Parmesan cheese

¼ cup minced fresh cilantro

serves 6

In a large, heavy pot, heat the oil over medium heat. Add the onion and sauté until softened, about 5 minutes. Add the garlic and sauté for 1 minute. Leaving the oil in the pan, transfer to a food processor or blender and add the beans. Purée until smooth, adding a splash of chicken stock as needed to aid the puréeing. Pass the puréed beans through a medium-mesh sieve to remove any remaining bits of skin.

Heat the oil remaining in the pan over medium heat. Pour the puréed beans into the hot oil and simmer, uncovered, for 2 minutes. Add the epazote, if using, and the corn kernels and season with the bouillon granules and salt and pepper to taste. Stirring occasionally, simmer until the corn is tender, about 4 minutes. Add a bit more stock, if necessary.

To prepare the condiments, finely chop the onion and the fresh and canned chiles. Peel, pit, and dice the avocado. Set aside.

Ladle the soup into heated bowls and top with condiments of your choice.

COOK'S NOTE: This soup can accommodate a mixed group of vegetarians and carnivores by using vegetable stock in place of chicken stock.

I first tasted this unusual soup in the area around the agricultural town of Apatzingán. Its mild, sweet flavor is a perfect contrast to a spicy main course.

cold melon soup

Corn or peanut oil for frying

3 thin corn tortillas, cut into ½-inch (12-mm) squares

3 very ripe cantaloupes, halved and seeded

2 tablespoons unsalted butter

1 russet potato, peeled and cut into chunks

1 cup (250 ml) whole milk

1 tablespoon medium-dry sherry (optional)

Fine sea salt

White pepper

1 tablespoon fresh lime juice

serves 4–6

In a small frying pan, heat ½ inch (12 mm) oil over medium-high heat. When very hot, add the tortilla squares and fry, turning at least once, until golden brown, about 3 minutes. Transfer to paper towels to drain.

Using the small end of a melon baller, press deep into the flesh of a melon half, twist, and scoop out a whole ball. Repeat until there are about 16 balls and place these in the refrigerator chill. Cut the remaining melon flesh into chunks and purée in a blender until smooth.

In a saucepan over medium heat, melt the butter. Add the potato and cook for 3 minutes, stirring constantly. Add the milk, cover, and simmer over low heat until the potato is soft, about 10 minutes. Let cool slightly, then purée in a blender or food processor. Return to the pan over medium heat and add ½ cup (125 ml) water, stirring constantly. Let the soup come to a slow boil. Add all but ½ cup (125 ml) of the puréed melon, the sherry (if using), 1 teaspoon salt, and ¼ teaspoon white pepper. Simmer over low heat, stirring often, for 10 minutes. Add the lime juice and remaining melon purée, stir well, and heat through.

Ladle into warmed bowls, garnish with the melon balls and crispy tortilla squares, and serve.

Mexican soups are substantial and filling: a meal, rather than an appetizer. These chopped shrimp *albondigas*, or meatballs, are delicately tinted with green herbs, spiked with fresh lemon, and served in a homemade broth with fine pasta known as *fideos*—an homage to tradition that is very quick to put together.

shrimp albondigas in tomatillo broth

FOR THE ALBONDIGAS

Oil for greasing, if needed

4 green onions, white and tender green parts, minced

1 clove garlic, sliced

½ bunch fresh cilantro, roughly chopped

2 large fresh epazote leaves, shredded

1 lb (500 g) shrimp, peeled, deveined, and patted dry

1 large egg white

½ cup (80 g) Seasoned White Rice (page 177) or Red Rice with Achiote (page 123)

1 teaspoon finely grated lemon zest

FOR THE SOUP

2 tablespoons vegetable oil

2 cups (150 g) dried *fideo* noodles or angel hair pasta, broken into pieces

1 teaspoon minced garlic

1 large plum tomato, seeded and diced

12 cups (3 qt/3 L) chicken stock, preferably homemade (page 173), heated

8 sprigs fresh cilantro, roughly chopped

Lemon wedges, for serving

serves 4–6

Preheat the oven to 350°F (180°C). Line two baking sheets with parchment paper, or lightly grease with oil.

To make the *albondigas,* combine the green onions, garlic, cilantro, and epazote in a food processor and pulse until well chopped. Add the shrimp and egg white and pulse until the shrimp are mostly chopped into large pieces, with some texture. Scrape into a bowl and stir in the rice and lemon zest. Use a tablespoon measure to scoop out heaping tablespoons of the mixture onto the prepared baking sheets. Form into balls with dampened hands. You will have about 20 *albondigas*. (At this point, the *albondigas* can be refrigerated until ready to cook.) Cover the baking sheets with aluminum foil and bake until springy to the touch, 10–12 minutes.

To make the soup, heat the oil in a Dutch oven or wide, heavy saucepan over medium heat. Add the *fideos,* garlic, and tomato, and cook until the noodles are lightly browned. Add the hot chicken stock, cilantro, and the *albondigas*. Simmer until the noodles are soft and the *albondigas* heated through, about 2 minutes.

Divide among warmed large soup bowls, arranging the *albondigas* on top. Squeeze a lemon wedge over each bowl, then serve.

Habas are rich and buttery smooth when cooked and puréed. The secret to this soup is an aromatic base of tomatoes, garlic, and onions—called a *recaudo*—that is puréed and sautéed before the beans are added to the pot.

fava bean soup

2 cups (14 oz/400 g) dried shelled fava beans (see Cook's Note)

1 plum tomato, roughly chopped

1 clove garlic, roughly chopped

1 small white onion, roughly chopped

Fine sea salt and freshly ground black pepper

1 tablespoon olive oil

¼ teaspoon crushed saffron threads (optional)

¼ teaspoon ground cumin

Roughly chopped fresh cilantro, to garnish

Fire-Roasted Tomato Salsa (page 144), to garnish (optional)

serves 4

Bring the fava beans and 4 cups (1 qt/1 L) water to a boil in a 4-qt (4-L) saucepan over high heat. Reduce the heat to medium-low and cook, covered and stirring occasionally, until tender, about 40 minutes.

Meanwhile, combine the tomato, garlic, and half of the onion in a blender or food processor and purée until smooth to make a *recaudo*. Season to taste with salt and pepper, and set aside.

Heat the oil in another 4-qt (4-L) saucepan over medium-high heat. Add the *recaudo* and cook, stirring constantly, until it begins to thicken, about 5 minutes.

Add the fava beans along with their cooking liquid, saffron (if using), and cumin. Bring to a boil, reduce the heat to medium, and cook, stirring occasionally, until the flavors meld and the beans are very tender and break up in the soup, about 10 minutes. Divide the soup among individual bowls and sprinkle with the remaining onions and the cilantro. Drizzle with salsa, if you like, before serving.

COOK'S NOTE: Make sure to purchase dried fava beans with the skins removed; the package label should clearly indicate whether or not it has been. Fava beans in their skins take twice as long to cook and need to be peeled once they're done.

The rambunctious flavor of the smoky chipotle chile in this classic soup, *caldo tlalpeño*, is tamed by the addition of earthy chickpeas. Its name refers to a district of Mexico City that traces its roots as an agricultural center back to pre-Hispanic times.

chicken & chickpea stew

6 cups (1½ qt/1.5 L) chicken stock, preferably homemade (page 173)

1 whole chicken breast, skinned

1 sprig fresh mint

1 tablespoon safflower or canola oil

½ large white onion, chopped

1 large carrot, peeled and diced

2 cloves garlic, chopped

1 canned chipotle chile in adobo, finely chopped

1 sprig fresh epazote

Fine sea salt and freshly ground black pepper

1 can (15 oz/425 g) chickpeas, drained and rinsed

1 avocado, preferably Hass, pitted, peeled, and diced

1 lime, cut into 6 wedges

serves 6

In a saucepan over medium heat, bring the stock, chicken, and mint to a simmer and cook, partially covered, until the chicken is opaque throughout, about 15 minutes. Using tongs, lift out the chicken and mint and reserve the cooking liquid. Discard the mint. Let the chicken cool until it can be handled, then bone the chicken and shred the meat. Set aside.

In a large saucepan, heat the oil over medium heat. Add the onion and carrot and sauté until the onion is translucent, about 5 minutes. Add the garlic and sauté for 1 minute longer. Pour in the reserved chicken cooking liquid and add the chipotle, epazote, ½ teaspoon salt, and ½ teaspoon pepper. Bring to a simmer, cover, and cook for 20 minutes. Stir in the chickpeas and simmer, uncovered, 10 minutes longer. Add the shredded chicken and heat through.

Ladle the soup into warmed bowls, top with the avocado, and pass the lime wedges at the table.

The most widely used Mexican chile is the large poblano, which has a distinctive flavor and a touch of heat. This hearty soup balances the chile with sweet corn, thick *crema*, and cheese, and adds more flavor with a sautéed mushroom garnish. All three vegetable ingredients were staples of ancient Aztec cuisine.

creamy poblano chile soup with corn & mushrooms

1 tablespoon safflower or canola oil

1 white onion, coarsely chopped

2 cloves garlic

2 cups (360 g) fresh or frozen corn kernels

3 poblano chiles, roasted, peeled, and seeded (page 178), then coarsely chopped

4 cups (1 qt/1 L) chicken stock, preferably homemade (page 173)

½ teaspoon dried oregano, preferably Mexican

2 tablespoons unsalted butter

8 oz (250 g) fresh chanterelle, cremini, or other flavorful mushrooms, brushed clean and sliced

Fine sea salt and freshly ground black pepper

½ cup (125 ml) *crema*, preferably homemade (page 177), or sour cream, thinned with whole milk

3 oz (90 g) Muenster cheese or farmers' cheese (see Cook's Note), at room temperature, cut into ¼-inch (6-mm) cubes or crumbled

serves 6

In a Dutch oven, *cazuela,* or other large pot, heat the safflower oil over medium-low heat. Add the onion and sauté until golden and soft, about 2 minutes. Add the garlic and cook for 1 minute longer. Raise the heat to medium and add 1 cup (180 g) of the corn, half of the chiles, and 1 cup (250 ml) of the chicken stock. Bring to a simmer, stir in the oregano, and cook, uncovered, until the corn is tender, 10–15 minutes. Remove from the heat and let cool slightly.

Ladle the corn mixture into a blender with ½ cup (125 ml) of the chicken stock and process until smooth. Pass the mixture through a medium-mesh sieve back into the pot. Add the remaining 2½ cups (600 ml) stock and bring to a simmer over medium-low heat.

While the soup is heating, in a frying pan, melt the butter over medium heat. Add the remaining poblano chiles, the remaining corn, and the mushrooms and stir well. Season to taste with salt and pepper and sauté until the mushrooms release their liquid and their liquid evaporates, about 8 minutes (or longer if you are using cremini).

Add the mushroom mixture and the *crema* to the soup, stir well, cover, and simmer for 10 minutes to blend the flavors. Taste and adjust the seasoning. Ladle the soup into warmed bowls and garnish with the cheese. Serve at once.

COOK'S NOTE: Farmers' cheese is a white, crumbly, fresh form of cottage cheese from which most of the liquid has been removed. It is sold in a fairly solid loaf shape and is mild and slightly tangy. It is a nice alternative to Muenster cheese, which is more of a melting cheese, for this soup.

Pozole, a hearty pork and hominy soup, is made all over Mexico with slight variations. You can turn this into *pozole verde* by replacing the tomatoes with tomatillos. Traditionally made with partially cooked and cleaned hominy *(nixtamal)*, this quick version uses canned white hominy. The pozole is also delicious made with chicken in place of pork.

pork & hominy stew

2 tablespoons corn oil or canola oil

1 lb (500 g) pork shoulder, cut into ½-inch (12-mm) pieces

1 yellow onion, finely chopped

3 cloves garlic, minced

1½ tablespoons chili powder

½ teaspoon ground cumin

½ teaspoon dried oregano

3 cups (700 ml) chicken stock, preferably homemade (page 173)

1 can (14.5 oz/400 g) diced fire-roasted tomatoes, with juices

1 can (15 oz/425 g) white hominy, rinsed and drained

1 jalapeño chile, seeded and diced

Fine sea salt and freshly ground black pepper

FOR SERVING

Avocado slices

Sliced green onions

Lime wedges

Corn tortillas, preferably homemade (page 106), warmed (optional)

serves 4

In a soup pot, heat the oil over medium heat. Working in batches, add the pork and sauté until opaque on all sides but not browned, about 3 minutes per batch. Transfer the meat to a bowl and set aside.

Add the onion to the same pot over medium heat and sauté until softened, 3–5 minutes. Add the garlic, chili powder, cumin, and oregano and cook, stirring to blend the spices evenly, about 1 minute longer.

Add the stock, tomatoes, hominy, jalapeño, sautéed pork with any juices, season with salt and pepper, and bring to a boil over high heat. Reduce the heat to low, cover, and simmer until the pork is cooked through and the soup is fragrant, about 15 minutes.

Ladle the soup into warmed bowls and garnish with the avocado slices and green onions; serve right away with the lime wedges and warm tortillas alongside, if desired.

Throughout northern and parts of central Mexico, pieces of tripe are simmered in a rich pork broth to become that popular restorative soup called *menudo*. With all of the condiments that are heaped on top, it serves as a full meal, traditionally on Sunday, after a night of carousing.

hominy & tripe stew

2 lb (1 kg) honeycomb tripe

1 tablespoon cider vinegar

2 pig's feet or 1 calf's foot, split lengthwise

1 lb (500 g) packaged freshly prepared pozole or 2 cans (14 oz/400 g each) white hominy, drained and rinsed

½ white onion, finely diced

4 bay leaves

3 cloves garlic

1 tablespoon dried oregano, preferably Mexican

Fine sea salt

3 dried ancho chiles, seeded and toasted (page 178), then soaked in very hot water for 30 minutes

2 tablespoons safflower or canola oil

FOR THE CONDIMENTS

6 limes, quartered

¼ cup (20 g) ground pequín chile or 3 serrano chiles, chopped

½ white onion, chopped

3 tablespoons dried oregano, preferably Mexican

serves 8 generously

Wash the tripe under running cold water and cut into ½-inch (12-mm) squares. Put them into a large pot and add the vinegar and water to cover. Bring to a slow boil over medium-high heat and simmer, uncovered, for 10 minutes. Drain, rinse the tripe, and return to the pot. Add the pig's feet or calf's foot and 10 cups (2½ qt/2.5 L) water. If using the freshly prepared pozole, add it to the pot. Bring to a boil over medium-high heat, skimming off any foam from the surface. Add the onion, bay leaves, garlic, oregano, and 1 teaspoon salt. Reduce the heat, cover, and simmer until both the tripe and the pozole are tender, 2–4 hours.

While the meat is cooking, drain the chiles, reserving the liquid. Tear the chiles into small pieces and put into a blender along with ½ cup (125 ml) of the soaking liquid. Blend until smooth, adding more liquid if necessary.

In a frying pan, heat the oil over medium-high heat. Pour in the puréed chiles and cook, stirring constantly, for several minutes. Ladle in 1 cup (250 ml) liquid from the simmering meat, reduce the heat, and simmer for 5 minutes. Add the chile sauce to the tripe. If using canned hominy, add it at this time as well.

Remove the pig's feet or calf's foot and skim off any excess fat from the surface of the menudo. When the pig's feet or calf's foot is cool enough to handle, cut off any meaty pieces and return them to the pot, discarding the bone and cartilage. Continue simmering for another 10–15 minutes to heat through and blend the flavors. The menudo is even tastier if prepared to this point several days in advance and refrigerated in a tightly sealed container. When ready to finish, remove any congealed fat and reheat.

Ladle the soup into warmed deep bowls. Set out small bowls of the condiments and let everyone choose their own toppings.

This classic comfort dish, whose name means "dry noodle soup," is less of a soup and more of a casserole or pasta dish, where the "soup" is a flavorful chile sauce that is absorbed into the thin *fideo* noodles. Serve it with a fresh salad such as Mixed Greens with Hearts of Palm, Red Onion & Avocado (page 105) alongside.

sopa seca de fideos

¼ cup (50 ml) olive oil, plus more for greasing

12 oz (350 g) dried *fideo* noodles or angel hair pasta, broken into 3-inch (7.5-mm) lengths (see Cook's Note)

1 medium white onion, thinly sliced

1 teaspoon ground coriander

¼ teaspoon cumin seeds

1 teaspoon dried oregano, preferably Mexican

1 teaspoon chili powder

6 cloves garlic, minced

1 bay leaf

1 can (14.5 oz/400 g) crushed tomatoes

3 canned chipotle chiles in adobo, minced

1 sprig fresh cilantro, plus 1 tablespoon minced, for garnish

2 cups (500 ml) chicken stock, preferably homemade (page 173)

Fine sea salt and freshly ground black pepper

1 cup (4 oz/100 g) crumbled cotija or feta cheese

1 cup (250 ml) *crema,* preferably homemade (page 177), or sour cream

serves 8

Heat the oven to 375°F (190°C). Grease an 8-inch (20-cm) square baking dish; set aside. Heat the ¼ cup (50 ml) oil in a 12-inch (30-cm) frying pan over medium-high heat. Working in two batches, add the pasta and cook, stirring, until lightly browned and toasted, about 4 minutes. Using a slotted spoon, transfer to paper towels to drain; set aside.

Return the frying pan to medium-high heat, add the onion, and cook, stirring, until soft, about 4 minutes. Add the coriander, cumin, oregano, chili powder, garlic, and bay leaf and cook, stirring, until fragrant, about 30 seconds. Add the tomatoes, chipotles, and cilantro sprig and cook until thickened, about 5 minutes. Add the reserved noodles and the stock, season with salt and pepper, and bring to a boil. Reduce the heat to medium-low and cook, stirring, until the noodles are al dente, about 6 minutes. Remove from the heat and pour into the prepared dish. Sprinkle with cheese and bake until the cheese is soft, about 15 minutes.

Drizzle with *crema,* sprinkle with minced cilantro, and serve.

COOK'S NOTE: Any long, thin, broken-up pasta will work here, including spaghetti.

Toward the Texas border, hearty cowboy cooking is the rule.
I love this combination of rich pork carnitas, sharp añejo cheese,
and crunchy *chicharrones*. This is a true *sopa seca*—a thick pasta
dish made with *fideos* (similar to angel hair pasta) that you build
right in one pot with leftover carnitas from taco night.

fideos norteños with carnitas & queso añejo

1 can (14.5 oz/400 g) diced tomatoes, with juices

2 medium tomatillos, husked and rinsed

½ cup (75 g) diced white onion, plus more for serving

1 large clove garlic

Fine sea salt

2 tablespoons vegetable oil

4 oz (120 g) dried *fideo* noodles or angel hair pasta, broken roughly into pieces (1½ cups)

1½ cups (350 ml) chicken stock, preferably homemade (page 173), heated

12 large fresh epazote leaves, shredded

8 sprigs fresh flat-leaf parsley or cilantro, chopped

About 2 cups (8 oz/250 g) carnitas (page 24)

¾ cup (3 oz/90 g) grated queso añejo or Parmesan cheese

1 cup (70 g) pork *chicharrones* (fried pork belly or rinds), broken into small pieces

serves 4–6

Combine the tomatoes, tomatillos, onion, garlic, and ¾ teaspoon salt in a food processor or blender and pulse until very finely chopped.

In a wide, heavy pot (such as a Dutch oven), heat the oil over medium heat. Add the *fideos* and toast, stirring, until golden brown, 5–7 minutes.

Add the puréed tomato mixture and cook, stirring often, until the *fideos* have absorbed most of the tomatoes, about 5 minutes more. Add the chicken stock, *fideos*, and all but 3 tablespoons of the epazote and parsley. Bring to a simmer and cook, stirring often, until the *fideos* are soft. The *sopa* will be thick. Taste and adjust the seasoning (remembering that the cheese will add salt).

Divide among warmed bowls or plates. Divide the carnitas, cheese, and *chicharrones* over the top and sprinkle with chopped herbs. Offer diced onions on the side.

COOK'S NOTE: This recipe may be halved, but have extra stock on hand— you may need slightly more than half the quantity.

This colorful rice is usually cooked and served in a clay *cazuela* as a substantial side dish alongside grilled chicken or meat, such as Lamb Chops with Pasilla Chile Sauce (page 94) or Grilled Beef Cecina (page 93). It also makes a tasty main dish.

fiesta rice

3 tablespoons safflower or canola oil, plus more for greasing

½ white onion, thinly sliced

4 poblano chiles, roasted, peeled, and seeded (page 178), then cut lengthwise into narrow strips

4 cups (640 g) Seasoned White Rice (page 177), at room temperature

½ cup (90 g) frozen or lightly cooked fresh corn kernels

2 cups (500 ml) *crema,* preferably homemade (page 177), or sour cream

Fine sea salt and freshly ground black pepper

½ teaspoon dried oregano, preferably Mexican

1 cup (250 ml) whole milk

8 oz (250 g) Manchego or Monterey Jack cheese, shredded (about 2 cups)

serves 6

Preheat the oven to 325°F (160°C). Grease a shallow 1½-qt (1.5-L) baking dish, such as an attractive ovenproof ceramic dish.

In a frying pan, heat the oil over medium heat. Add the onion and sauté until just translucent, about 3 minutes. Stir in the chile strips and sauté, stirring occasionally, for about 10 minutes.

Spoon half of the rice into the bottom of the prepared baking dish, spreading it in an even layer. Spread half of the onion-chile mixture and half of the corn over the rice, then drizzle half of the *crema* on top. Season with salt and pepper and the oregano. Repeat the layering with the remaining rice, onion-chile mixture, and *crema.* Pour the milk evenly over the top and sprinkle with the cheese.

Bake the rice until the cheese is bubbling hot, about 20 minutes. Serve hot, directly from the dish.

Whether it's called *pollo con arroz* or *arroz con pollo*, this dish is all about the flavor of the rice. Seasonings differ slightly from region to region, but the dish is always built on a colorful *sofrito* of peppers and onions, which imbues the rice with a vibrant hue and flavor.

arroz con pollo

4 large cloves garlic, minced

2 teaspoons red pepper flakes

1 tablespoon white vinegar

Fine sea salt and freshly ground black pepper

1 chicken, about 3½ lb (1.6 kg), cut into 8 serving pieces

3 tablespoons olive oil

1 qt (1 L) chicken stock, preferably homemade (page 173)

½ teaspoon saffron threads

1 red onion, diced

1 red bell pepper, seeded and diced

1 green bell pepper, seeded and diced

1 large jalapeño chile, seeded and minced

4 plum tomatoes, diced

1 teaspoon ground cumin

2 bay leaves

2 cups (14 oz/400 g) uncooked long-grain white rice

serves 6

In a bowl, combine the garlic, red pepper flakes, vinegar, 1 teaspoon salt, and ½ teaspoon black pepper and stir to mix well. Add the chicken pieces and toss to coat with the marinade. Refrigerate for at least 1 hour and up to overnight.

In a large sauté pan or large, shallow flameproof casserole dish with a tight-fitting lid, heat the olive oil over medium heat. Remove the chicken from the marinade, reserving the marinade, and arrange skin side down in the pan. Cook the chicken without turning until golden brown on the first side, 10–15 minutes. Turn the chicken, cover the pan, and cook until golden brown on the second side, about 10 minutes longer.

Meanwhile, in a saucepan over medium-high heat, heat the stock until steaming. Remove from the heat, add the saffron, and set aside to steep.

Transfer the chicken to a plate and pour off all but 2 tablespoons fat from the pan. Add the onion, red and green bell peppers, and jalapeño and sauté until softened, about 3 minutes. Add the tomatoes and cook, stirring, for 1 minute. Add the cumin, bay leaves, and the rice and cook, stirring constantly, until the rice grains are translucent and have absorbed the fats and juices in the pan, 3–5 minutes.

Pour the reserved marinade and saffron-infused stock into the pan and stir briefly. Place the chicken on top and drizzle in any juices that accumulated on the plate. Raise the heat to medium-high and bring to a boil. Reduce the heat to low, cover, and simmer until the chicken is opaque throughout, the rice is tender, and all the liquid has been absorbed, about 25 minutes. Taste and adjust the seasoning. Discard the bay leaves.

Remove from the heat, uncover partially, and let rest for 5–10 minutes. Serve right away, directly from the pan.

COOK'S NOTE: *Arroz con pollo* is traditionally cooked on the stove top, so the pan is important; it should be wide and shallow, rather than deep, with a tight-fitting lid. A large frying pan with a lid is ideal.

This recipe from Tabasco is similar to one from nearby Campeche, where oysters are often substituted for the clams. There, sautéed bell peppers are usually added for color and a slightly different flavor. Either way, it's a thoroughly Mexican take on Spanish paella.

saffron rice with clams

Large pinch of saffron threads

3 tablespoons hot water

3 cups (700 ml) warm water, plus warm water to cover rice

2 cups (400 g) medium- or long-grain white rice

2 ripe tomatoes, about 10 oz (300 g), cut into chunks, or 1 can (14.5 oz/400 g) diced tomatoes, drained

¼ cup (30 g) chopped white onion

2 teaspoons chopped garlic (about 6 small cloves)

⅓ cup (75 ml) safflower or canola oil

2 lb (1 kg) small clams, well scrubbed

4 sprigs fresh flat-leaf parsley, chopped

Fine sea salt

serves 6–8

In a small bowl, soak the saffron threads in the hot water for about 10 minutes. In a medium bowl, soak the rice in warm water to cover for 10 minutes. Drain the rice and rinse under running cold water until the water runs clear. Drain thoroughly. Put the tomatoes in a blender. Add the onion, garlic, and saffron with its soaking water. Process until smooth.

In a *cazuela* or heavy saucepan, heat the oil over medium heat. Stir in the rice and sauté until golden, about 5 minutes. Pour the tomato mixture through a sieve placed over the saucepan. Simmer, stirring occasionally, to combine the flavors, 6–8 minutes. Put the 3 cups (700 ml) warm water into the unrinsed blender, swirl it around, and add to the rice. Bring to a boil and add the clams, discarding any that do not close to the touch, parsley, and 2 teaspoons salt. Stir once, cover, and simmer over low heat until the rice is fluffy and the clams have opened, 20–25 minutes.

Spoon the rice and clams into a wide, shallow serving bowl or into individual plates with rims, discarding any clams that failed to open. Serve at once.

main dishes

Quickly made from simple ingredients on hand, chilaquiles are a terrific way to use up old tortillas or dregs of salsa. The sauce for this version is made with fresh tomatillos and spiked with fresh green chiles. Chilaquiles are usually served with eggs or meats and a side of creamy black beans to make a colorful and hearty dish.

chilaquiles with poached eggs

2 tablespoons sunflower, grapeseed, or canola oil

2 cups (500 ml) Tomatillo Sauce (page 174) or Red Chile Sauce (page 174)

1 cup (250 ml) chicken stock, preferably homemade (page 173)

Fine sea salt and freshly ground black pepper

2 cups (500 ml) safflower or canola oil

18 day-old corn tortillas, 6 inches (15 cm) in diameter, torn or cut into strips

½ small yellow onion, chopped

4 oz (100 g) Monterey Jack cheese, shredded (about 1 cup)

2 tablespoons chopped fresh oregano

1 teaspoon fresh lemon juice

4–6 large eggs

4 oz (100 g) queso fresco or fresh goat cheese, crumbled

Hot sauce, for serving (optional)

serves 4

In a large saucepan, heat the sunflower oil over medium heat. Add the tomatillo sauce and cook, stirring, until the sauce darkens, 4–5 minutes. Gradually add the stock and continue to cook, stirring occasionally, until a medium-thick sauce forms, about 10 minutes longer. Stir in ½ teaspoon salt and ½ teaspoon pepper and set aside.

In a heavy frying pan, heat the safflower oil over medium-high heat to 375°F (190°C) on a deep-frying thermometer. (If you don't have a thermometer, dip the edge of a tortilla into the oil; it should sizzle immediately and vigorously.) Working in batches, add the tortilla strips and fry until golden on one side, about 30 seconds. Turn and fry until golden on the second side, 15–20 seconds. Transfer to paper towels to drain.

Pour off all but 1–2 teaspoons of the oil from the pan and place over medium heat. Add the onion and cook, stirring, until translucent, about 1 minute. Add the tortilla strips and the tomatillo sauce and cook, stirring gently, until the chips are soft, 3–4 minutes. Stir in the cheese and half of the oregano. Continue to cook until the cheese has melted, 4–5 minutes longer. Remove from the heat and stir in the remaining oregano.

Pour 2 inches (5 cm) of water into a large saucepan and add the lemon juice. Place over medium heat and bring to a gentle simmer. Break an egg into a small bowl, making sure the yolk doesn't break. Gently slide the egg into the simmering water. Repeat with the remaining eggs, spacing them about 1 inch (2.5 cm) apart. Keep the water at a gentle simmer. Cook until the whites are set, 4–5 minutes.

Just before the eggs are done, divide the chilaquiles among four plates. Using a slotted spoon, lift each egg from the water, letting the excess water drain into the pan. Trim any ragged edges of egg white with kitchen scissors. Top each serving of chilaquiles with a poached egg and some of the queso fresco. Serve right away, with hot sauce, if desired.

Mexican cooks have a special way with vegetables. *Dulce de calabasa*, both spicy and lightly sweet, inspired this vegetarian taco of roasted winter squash and caramelized onions fragrant with chiles and cumin. It is enhanced with a smoky red pepper salsa. The taco is vegan if the cheese is omitted.

roast butternut squash tacos with caramelized onion

FOR THE SQUASH

1 medium butternut squash, seeded, peeled, and diced into 1-inch (2.5-cm) cubes

½ medium white onion, thinly sliced into half-moons

¼ cup (50 ml) vegetable oil

Fine sea salt and freshly ground black pepper

1 teaspoon ground cumin

1 teaspoon Spanish smoked paprika

1 teaspoon ancho chile powder

2 tablespoons brown sugar

FOR SERVING

Corn tortillas, preferably homemade (page 106)

2 cups (8 oz/225 g) shredded Menonita, Oaxaca, or Monterey Jack cheese

Smoky Red Pepper Salsa (page 140)

Avocado slices

Bottled hot sauce

Diced white onion mixed with chopped fresh cilantro (optional)

makes 12–16 small tacos

To prepare the squash, preheat the oven to 375°F (190°C). In a bowl, mix the cubed squash, onion, oil, 2 teaspoons salt, 1 teaspoon black pepper, the cumin, paprika, ancho chile, and brown sugar until well coated. Spread in a single layer on a rimmed baking sheet and roast until soft and well caramelized, 25–30 minutes.

Heat a heavy griddle and lightly grease the surface. Cook the tortillas, topped with a pinch of the cheese, until the cheese is melted and the tortilla is slightly crisp. Top each with about ¼ cup of roasted squash, a spoonful of the salsa, and a slice of avocado. Serve with the bottled hot sauce and onion mixture (if using) for diners to fix their own.

This dish from coastal Mexico pairs plump, sweet shrimp with a bright sauce of fresh orange juice and a dash of fresh green chile. It's so simple and quick—perfect for a weeknight meal. A squeeze of lime juice adds another level of flavor to the seasoned rice.

shrimp with orange & tequila

1 navel orange

6 tablespoons (90 g) unsalted butter

2 tablespoons finely chopped white onion

2 cloves garlic

16 large shrimp, peeled and deveined, with tail segments intact

1 canned chipotle in adobo or 2 serrano chiles, finely chopped

¼ cup (50 ml) tequila *reposado*

3 tablespoons coarsely chopped fresh cilantro

Fine sea salt

Seasoned White Rice (page 177) or Coconut Rice (page 177), for serving

serves 4

With a zester or vegetable peeler, cut the zest from the orange in very narrow strips, being careful to avoid any of the bitter white pith. If the strips are too wide, cut them lengthwise into ¼-inch (6-mm) strips.

Bring a saucepan of water to a boil over high heat. Place the orange strips in a small sieve and plunge them into the boiling water. Remove immediately and rinse under running cold water. Repeat three times to remove the bitter taste. Pat the orange strips dry with paper towels.

In a frying pan, melt the butter over medium heat. Add the onion and sauté until translucent, 3–4 minutes. Add the garlic and shrimp and cook, stirring frequently, until the shrimp turn pink and begin to curl, 4–5 minutes. Add the chipotle chile and orange strips to the pan, stirring briefly to mix. Pour the tequila over the shrimp, carefully ignite with a long match, and let the flames burn out.

Remove from the heat, stir in the cilantro, and season to taste with salt. Spoon the rice onto a warmed platter or individual plates and top with the shrimp and some of the remaining sauce from the pan. Serve right away.

Traditionally, this rustic layered tortilla dish known as *torta azteca* would use the much-esteemed *huitlacoche*, a delicious edible fungus that grows on corn, but any type of mushroom will contribute the needed earthy flavor.

savory layered tortilla cake

1 large chicken breast half

¼ cup (30 g) coarsely chopped white onion, plus 1 thick slice

2 cloves garlic

Fine sea salt and freshly ground black pepper

1 lb (500 g) tomatoes, roasted (page 178) and quartered, or 1 can (14.5 oz/ 400 g) diced tomatoes, with juices

3 serrano chiles, coarsely chopped

1 teaspoon safflower or canola oil, plus more for greasing

8 thin corn tortillas, each cut into 6 wedges, or 48–50 unsalted tortilla chips

1 tablespoon unsalted butter

4 oz (120 g) mushrooms, brushed clean and sliced

2 poblano chiles, roasted, peeled, and seeded (page 178), then sliced (optional, but highly recommended)

⅔ cup (5½ oz/160 g) *crema*, preferably homemade (page 177), or sour cream

½ cup (2 oz/60 g) shredded queso Chihuahua or Monterey Jack cheese

6 radishes, thinly sliced

serves 4

Place the chicken in a saucepan with the onion slice, one of the garlic cloves, and ½ teaspoon salt. Add water to cover and bring to a boil. Reduce the heat to medium, cover, and simmer for 15–20 minutes. Lift out the chicken and shred the meat, discarding the skin and bones. Reserve the cooking liquid, skimming off any fat from the surface.

In a blender or food processor, purée the tomatoes with the chiles, chopped onion, and remaining garlic clove. In a small saucepan, heat the oil over medium heat until smoking. Add the tomato mixture and fry, stirring occasionally, until the color darkens, 3–4 minutes. Add ½ cup (125 ml) of the reserved cooking liquid and season with salt and pepper. Bring the sauce to a boil, reduce the heat to medium-low, and simmer, uncovered, until thickened, 8–10 minutes. Remove from the heat and keep warm.

Preheat the oven to 350°F (180°C). Lightly grease an 8-inch (20-cm) square baking dish.

If using tortillas, place the wedges in a single layer on a baking sheet and cover with a wire rack to keep them from curling. Bake for about 10 minutes, then set aside. Leave the oven on.

In a small frying pan, melt the butter over medium-high heat. Add the mushrooms and sauté until any liquid evaporates, 5–8 minutes.

Put one-third of the tortilla wedges or chips in the bottom of the baking dish. Top with half of the poblano chiles (if using), chicken, mushrooms, and *crema*. Spoon on one-third of the sauce and cheese. Top with half of the remaining tortilla wedges or chips and add the remaining chiles, chicken, mushrooms, and *crema*. Top with half of the remaining sauce and cheese. Finish with the remaining tortilla wedges or chips and the remaining sauce and cheese.

Bake until the sauce starts to bubble and all the layers are heated through, 15–20 minutes. Remove from the oven, scatter the radish slices on top, and serve immediately directly from the dish.

Esquites is my favorite Mexican street food: grilled sweet corn, cut from the cob and tossed with spicy mayonnaise, fresh lime, and cotija cheese. I've turned it into a warm entrée salad combined with spicy sautéed shrimp, peppery arugula, and fresh lemon. Start to finish, this can be on the table in less than half an hour.

grilled corn & shrimp salad

FOR THE CORN & SHRIMP

2 ears fresh sweet corn, husks and silks removed

2 tablespoons olive oil

1 lb (500 g) medium shrimp, peeled and deveined

2 teaspoons minced garlic

Fine sea salt

¼ cup (50 g) chipotle chiles in adobo (or to taste), puréed

¼ cup (15 g) fresh cilantro leaves, roughly chopped

FOR THE SALAD

1 lb (500 g) wild arugula leaves (about 12 cups), chilled

¼–⅓ cup (50–75 ml) best-quality extra-virgin olive oil

2 lemons, halved, plus 4 lemon wedges, for serving

½ cup (2 oz/60 g) grated cotija, cotija enchilado, queso añejo, or Romano cheese

¾ cup (6½ oz/190 g) *pico de gallo* salsa, preferably homemade (page 129), or seeded and diced plum tomatoes

2 whole pickled jalapeño chiles, seeded and cut lengthwise into strips

serves 4

To prepare the corn and shrimp, heat a heavy frying pan over high heat until very hot. Hold the shucked ear of corn upright on a cutting board or in a small bowl and, using a sharp knife, cut off the kernels, keeping the blade angled inward so you get the whole kernel but none of the tough cob. Toss the kernels with 1 tablespoon of the olive oil. Add the corn to the hot pan in one layer and allow it to sear without stirring, then remove from the pan. (Some kernels may pop.)

Place the same pan over medium heat, add the remaining 1 tablespoon olive oil, and sauté the shrimp, garlic, and ¼ teaspoon salt until the shrimp just start to turn pink. Add the chipotle purée and cook and stir. Remove the pan from the heat and stir in the chopped cilantro and the seared corn. Set aside.

While the shrimp is cooking, make the salad. In a large bowl, toss the arugula with the olive oil and ¼ teaspoon salt. Squeeze the lemon halves over the greens, add the cheese and *pico de gallo,* and toss again.

Divide the salad among four plates. Top each with an equal amount of the corn and shrimp mixture, a couple strips of jalapeño, and a lemon wedge. Serve.

Mexican cooks stuff chiles of all types and sizes with a fantastic assortment of fillings. The chiles are often pan-roasted or grilled rather than breaded and fried. This simple, satisfying, and infinitely adaptable grilled chile is served with a fresh tomato sauce that has a spicy, smoky chipotle kick.

grilled chiles rellenos stuffed with shrimp rice

Arroz Verde (page 122) or Red Rice with Achiote (page 123)

Salsa Diabla (page 141)

4 large poblano chiles, roasted (page 178)

1 tablespoon olive oil

1 tablespoon butter

3 cloves garlic, finely minced

24 medium shrimp, peeled and deveined

Fine sea salt

1 plum tomato, seeded and finely diced

2 tablespoons minced fresh cilantro (about 3 sprigs)

⅔ cup (2½ oz/75 g) shredded Oaxaca, Menonita, or Monterey Jack cheese

2 tablespoons grated cotija or Romano cheese

serves 4

Make the rice and salsa. (The rice and salsa may be made a day or two in advance and refrigerated. Reheat the sauce just before serving; the rice can be used cold.)

After roasting the poblanos, carefully rub off the charred skin, being careful to keep the stem intact. Make a slit several inches long on one side, and with a small spoon, remove as many of the seeds as possible.

Heat a small sauté pan over medium heat. Add the olive oil and butter. When the butter is melted, add the garlic, shrimp, ¼ teaspoon salt, and the tomato, and cook, stirring, until the shrimp are firm and pink. Set aside to cool, then stir in the cilantro.

Preheat the oven to 350°F (180°C). Fill each chile with rice until the chile looks plump—about ½ cup (80 g) or more for a large chile. Sprinkle the exposed rice evenly with 2 tablespoons of the cheese. Lay 6 shrimp overlapping on the rice, making sure that a bit of tomato appears on top. Scatter one-fourth of the cotija cheese over the shrimp. Place the chile in a lightly oiled shallow baking dish just large enough to hold them all with a little space between. Repeat with the remaining chiles, then spoon what's left in the shrimp pan over the *chiles rellenos*. (The chiles may be refrigerated at this point until nearly ready to serve.)

Cover with foil and bake until an instant-read thermometer inserted into the rice reads 150°F (65°C), 10–15 minutes. Uncover, plate, and serve very hot with the *salsa diabla*.

COOK'S NOTE: If spicy heat is not your thing, substitute large Anaheim chiles for poblanos, and leave out the jalapeños and chipotles in the rice and salsa recipes. It will still be delicious.

Squid comes in many sizes, but the preferred type for this recipe is the diminutive *chipirone*, perhaps the smallest squid in the sea. Cooked quickly over very hot coals, they become meltingly tender. The versatile bean accompaniment is also delicious with sizzling hot-off-the-grill beef and other grilled meats.

grilled squid
with spicy black beans

2 tablespoons olive oil, plus more for greasing

1 small clove garlic, minced

½ teaspoon dried oregano, preferably Mexican

Coarse sea salt and freshly ground black pepper

1 lb (500 g) cleaned small squid, preferably extra-small chipirones

FOR THE BEANS

1 tablespoon olive oil

½ large yellow onion, thinly sliced

1 dry-cured chorizo sausage, about 5 inches (13 cm) long, thinly sliced

½ tomato, peeled, seeded, and diced

1 clove garlic, minced

¼ teaspoon seeded and minced habanero chile

½ teaspoon ground cumin

Fine sea salt and freshly ground black pepper

1½ cups (270 g) cooked black beans, rinsed (one 15-oz/425-g can)

Tomato-Avocado Salsa (page 128)

serves 4

Soak four 8-inch (20-cm) bamboo skewers in water to cover for 30 minutes.

In a baking dish, combine the olive oil, garlic, oregano, ½ teaspoon salt, and ½ teaspoon pepper and stir to mix well. Set aside. If the squid are larger than 1½ inches (4 cm) long, make cuts on the bodies of the squid just to score the flesh; do not cut through the body of the squid. Drain the skewers. Thread the squid lengthwise onto the skewers, dividing them evenly. Place the assembled skewers in the baking dish and turn to coat with the olive oil mixture. Set aside and let marinate at room temperature for at least 15 minutes.

To prepare the beans, in a sauté pan, heat the olive oil over medium heat. Add the onion and chorizo and cook, stirring often, until the onion is translucent and the chorizo lightly browned, about 5 minutes. Add the tomato, garlic, habanero, cumin, ½ teaspoon salt, and ½ teaspoon black pepper and cook until the tomato is tender and begins to break down, about 10 minutes. Add the beans and cook, stirring occasionally, until almost all of the liquid is absorbed and the mixture is the consistency of a thick sauce, about 10 minutes longer. Keep warm until ready to serve.

Build a fire in a charcoal grill for direct grilling over high heat, or preheat a gas grill to high. Generously oil the grill rack and position it 2–4 inches (5–10 cm) above the coals.

When the coals are very hot, arrange the skewers on the grill rack directly over the coals and, working quickly, grill just until the squid turns opaque and is nicely grill marked, up to 2 minutes per side.

To serve, spoon the beans onto a platter and arrange the squid on top. Serve right away with the salsa.

Casserole-like *tortas* are a common light supper dish in Mexico. This popular combination of zucchini, corn, and roasted poblano chile is the perfect thing to make in the summer, when fresh corn is at its peak. Poblano chiles have a wonderful flavor, but can be spicy. Mild California (dried Anaheim) chiles may be substituted.

zucchini & corn torta with cilantro-lime crema

Butter for greasing

1 ear white sweet corn, husk and silks removed

3 tablespoons olive oil

2 large poblano or California (dried Anaheim) chiles, roasted, peeled, and seeded (page 178), then cut into 1-inch (2.5-cm) pieces

1 white onion, chopped

Fine sea salt and freshly ground pepper

1 lb (500 g) zucchini, thinly sliced

½ teaspoon dried oregano, preferably Mexican, crumbled

1½ cups (6 oz/170 g) shredded Oaxacan or Monterey Jack cheese

4 large eggs, beaten

¼ cup (1 oz/30 g) crumbled cotija or feta cheese

¼ teaspoon ancho chile powder (optional)

Cilantro-Lime Crema (page 177), for serving

serves 4

Position a rack in the upper third of the oven and preheat to 325°F (160°C). Grease a 1½-qt (1.5-L) gratin dish or other shallow baking dish.

Holding the ear of corn upright on a cutting board, use a sharp knife to cut off the kernels, keeping the blade angled inward so you get the whole kernel but none of the cob. You should have about ¾ cup (130 g) kernels. Set aside.

In a frying pan, heat 1 tablespoon of the olive oil over medium heat. Add the chiles and onion and cook, stirring often, until the onion is tender, about 5 minutes. Stir in ½ teaspoon salt. Scrape into a colander to let drain and cool.

Add the remaining 2 tablespoons olive oil to the pan and return the pan to medium heat. Add the corn and zucchini and cook, stirring often, until the zucchini is softened but not breaking up, about 5 minutes. Stir in the oregano, ½ teaspoon salt, and ¼ teaspoon pepper and cook to blend the flavors, about 30 seconds. Add to the colander with the chiles. Let the cooked vegetables drain and cool for 15 minutes.

Spread 1 cup (180 g) of the zucchini mixture in an even layer in the bottom of the prepared dish. Sprinkle half of the Oaxacan cheese on top. Repeat to make a second layer of the vegetables, top with the remaining Oaxacan cheese, and end with the remaining vegetables.

Season the eggs with ½ teaspoon salt and a pinch of pepper. Pour into the dish and use a spatula to spread evenly. Scatter the cotija cheese over the top and dust with the chile powder. Bake until puffed and lightly browned, about 30 minutes.

Serve the torta warm or at room temperature with the *crema*.

The most famous of all of Veracruz's dishes is the silver-tinged, red-skinned *huachinango* snapper, caught in local waters and served with a colorful sauce of fresh tomatoes and herbs studded with Spanish olives and capers—the perfect crossroads of colonial and ancient Mexican cuisines.

veracruz-style red snapper

8 large cloves garlic

2 teaspoons fresh lime juice

Fine sea salt

6 skinless red snapper fillets, 5–6 oz (150–180 g) each

FOR THE SAUCE

¼ cup (50 ml) olive oil, plus more for greasing

1 large white onion, thinly sliced

4 large cloves garlic, minced

3 lb (1.5 kg) ripe tomatoes, roasted and peeled (page 178), then finely chopped

20 small green pimiento-stuffed olives, quartered

½ cup (30 g) coarsely chopped fresh flat-leaf parsley

3 bay leaves

3 pickled jalapeño chiles, cut lengthwise into strips, with 1 tablespoon pickling liquid

1 tablespoon capers

½ teaspoon *each* dried oregano, marjoram, and thyme, or 4 fresh sprigs each

Fine sea salt and freshly ground black pepper

serves 6

Using a mortar and pestle, mash the garlic to a paste and transfer to a small bowl, or squeeze it through a garlic press. Add the lime juice and ½ teaspoon salt and mix well.

Place the fish fillets on a large plate or in a baking dish. Rub the garlic mixture over both sides of each fillet. Cover the dish in plastic wrap and let it marinate in the refrigerator for at least 30 minutes or up to 2 hours, turning occasionally for even coating.

Preheat the oven to 350°F (180°C). In a large, heavy frying pan, heat the olive oil over medium heat. Add the onion and sauté until soft, about 4 minutes. Add the garlic and continue cooking until golden, 1–2 minutes. Raise the heat to medium-high, add the tomatoes, and continue cooking, stirring frequently, until the sauce thickens, 5–7 minutes. Reduce the heat to low and stir in the olives, parsley, bay leaves, jalapeños and their pickling liquid, and capers. Add the oregano, marjoram, and thyme and season to taste with salt and pepper. Simmer, stirring occasionally, until the flavors are well blended, 8–10 minutes.

Lightly oil a large glass or ceramic baking dish. Unwrap the fish, place in the dish, and spoon the sauce evenly over the top, discarding the bay leaves. Bake, basting occasionally with the sauce, just until the flesh is opaque throughout when tested in the thickest part, about 8–10 minutes. Serve directly from the baking dish or, using 2 spatulas, carefully transfer to a warmed platter.

Wild trout thrive in the mountain streams of Mexico, where they are often stuffed with herbs before cooking. The delicate flavor of trout stands up well to the bold flavors from the aromatics. A uniquely Mexican ingredient is dried avocado leaf, which has a mild licorice scent and flavor. Fresh tarragon is a good substitute.

trout with avocado sauce

4 whole boned trout, about 6 oz (180 g) each, cleaned, with heads intact or removed

Fine sea salt and freshly ground black pepper

¼ cup (25 g) thinly sliced red onion

3 cloves garlic, 2 cloves thinly sliced and 1 chopped

2 limes, thinly sliced

½ bunch fresh cilantro sprigs, tough stems removed, plus ¼ cup (15 g) chopped

2 dried avocado leaves (page 182) or 4 long sprigs fresh tarragon

3 tomatillos, husked and rinsed

1 large, ripe avocado, pitted, peeled, and cut into chunks

1 tablespoon minced white onion

1 clove garlic, chopped

2 tablespoons vegetable oil

¼ cup (30 g) all-purpose flour

FOR SERVING

Seasoned White Rice (page 177)

Lime wedges

serves 4

Rinse the trout and pat dry, inside and out. Season inside and out with salt and pepper. Stuff the cavities with the red onion, sliced garlic, sliced lime, and half of the cilantro sprigs, dividing all the ingredients evenly.

To toast the avocado leaves, using tongs, hold a leaf 2 inches (5 cm) above the flame of a gas burner on the stove top, passing each side quickly over the flame a few times until it turns a uniform brighter green. (If using an electric range, hold the leaf 4–6 inches/10–15 cm above the heat source.) Repeat to toast the second leaf. Crumble the toasted leaves into the cavities of the fish, dividing them evenly (or add 1 tarragon sprig to each). Close the trout. Cut 12 pieces of kitchen twine and tie each trout 3–4 times around the belly, gently but securely.

To make the avocado sauce, chop the tomatillos coarsely. In a blender or food processor, combine the tomatillos, avocado, white onion, garlic, chopped cilantro, and 1 teaspoon salt and process to a smooth purée, stopping to scrape down the sides as needed. Add ¼ cup (50 ml) water and pulse to combine. Add more water for a thinner sauce. Taste and adjust the seasoning.

In a large frying pan, heat the oil over medium heat. Spread the flour out on a large plate. When the oil is hot, lightly dredge each trout in the flour, shaking off any excess, and lay it in the pan. Cook until golden brown on the first side, about 7 minutes. Using tongs or 2 spatulas, carefully turn the fish and cook until the skins are golden on the second side and the flesh is opaque throughout, about 7 minutes longer. Serve the trout on individual plates and pass the avocado sauce, rice, and lime wedges.

COOK'S NOTE: A variation on this recipe is to wrap the stuffed trout in soaked corn husks. Tie with strips of the corn husk and grill the fish directly over a hot fire for 7 minutes per side.

A good *tinga* will always be full flavored and spicy. This version includes Mexican chorizo, a fresh sausage made with plenty of garlic and chiles, as well as the usual chipotles in adobo. It's terrific served with rice or as a taco filling.

tinga poblana with chicken

4 chicken thighs, bone in and skin on, about 1 lb (500 g) total weight

½ white onion, cut into chunks, plus 1 cup (150 g) finely chopped

4 cloves garlic, 2 cloves slightly smashed and 2 cloves finely chopped

Fine sea salt

1 tablespoon safflower or canola oil

8 oz (250 g) Mexican chorizo, casings removed and sausage crumbled

1 can (14.5 oz/400 g) diced tomatoes, drained

1 teaspoon dried oregano, preferably Mexican

2 bay leaves

2 canned chipotle chiles in adobo, plus 1 tablespoon sauce

FOR THE GARNISHES

½ white onion, quartered, thinly sliced crosswise, and separated into quarter-rings

2 ripe Hass avocados, pitted and peeled, then cut into ½-inch (12-mm) chunks

serves 6

Combine the chicken thighs, onion chunks, and smashed garlic in a saucepan and add water to cover. Add 1 teaspoon salt and bring to a boil over high heat, skimming off any foam that forms on the surface. Reduce the heat to medium-low and simmer, uncovered, until the chicken is opaque throughout, 20–30 minutes. Using tongs or a slotted spoon, transfer the chicken to a plate. Reserve the cooking liquid. When the chicken is cool enough to handle, remove and discard the skin and bones and coarsely shred the meat with your fingers.

In a large frying pan, Dutch oven, or *cazuela*, heat the safflower or canola oil over medium heat. Add the chorizo and fry for about 5 minutes. Discard the excess rendered fat from the pan, leaving just 1 tablespoon. Add the finely chopped onion and garlic and sauté until beginning to soften, but not yet starting to brown, about 1 minute. Add the shredded chicken, tomatoes, oregano, bay leaves, chiles and sauce, and about 1 cup (250 ml) of the reserved chicken cooking liquid to keep the mixture moist. Simmer, uncovered, until the flavors are blended, about 15 minutes. Add more liquid to the pan if the mixture begins to stick, but do not add too much; the mixture should absorb the liquid and not be runny. Remove and discard the bay leaves and season to taste with salt. Scoop the chicken into a warmed serving dish and garnish with the onion and avocado.

COOK'S NOTE: The chicken can be cooked up to 1 day in advance. Cover and refrigerate until needed. You can also prepare the entire dish 1–2 days in advance and then reheat it over low heat. Serve with warmed corn tortillas (page 106) for diners to use for making tacos, or spoon over white rice.

Moles are traditional Mexican sauces, usually reserved for important fiestas. The long list of ingredients produces a darkly complex sauce with a hint of sweetness. While the traditional process involves multiple steps and can seem daunting, this simplified version will have a festive dish on your table in no time.

quick chicken mole poblano

4 oz (100 g) dried pasilla chiles

10 cups (2½ qt/2.5 L) boiling water

1 whole chicken, 3–4 lb (1.5–2 kg), cut into 8 pieces

2 tablespoons butter

2 cloves garlic, chopped

½ plum tomato, chopped

½ tomatillo, husked, rinsed, and chopped

¼ small white onion, chopped

¼ teaspoon *each* ground cloves, allspice, cinnamon, coriander, aniseeds, and black pepper

2 tablespoons whole almonds

2 tablespoons raisins

1½ tablespoons sesame seeds, plus more for garnish

½ corn tortilla, torn

½ slice stale white bread, toasted and crumbled

¼ ripe plantain or banana, peeled and finely chopped

1 tablespoon safflower oil

2 oz (60 g) Mexican chocolate, roughly chopped

1 tablespoon light brown sugar

Fine sea salt

serves 8

Heat a 12-inch (30-cm) frying pan over medium-high heat. Add the chiles and cook, turning once, until toasted, about 2 minutes. Transfer the chiles to a large bowl; pour over boiling water and let sit until chiles soften, about 30 minutes. Drain, reserving the soaking liquid, and remove the stems and seeds, reserving 2 teaspoons seeds. Purée the chiles and 2 cups (500 ml) of the soaking liquid in a blender until smooth. Set the chile purée and remaining soaking liquid aside. Bring the chicken and 8 cups (2 qt/2 L) water to a boil in a 4-qt (4-L) saucepan over high heat, reduce heat to medium-low, and simmer until cooked through, about 30 minutes. Drain and keep warm.

Heat the butter in the same saucepan over medium-high heat. Add the garlic, tomato, tomatillo, and onion, and cook, stirring, until soft, about 8 minutes. Add the reserved chile seeds, cloves, allspice, cinnamon, coriander, anise, and pepper, and cook, stirring constantly, until fragrant, about 1 minute. Add the almonds, raisins, sesame seeds, tortilla, toast, and plantain, and cook, stirring, until lightly toasted, about 7 minutes. Add the reserved chile purée and bring to a boil; reduce the heat to medium-low and cook until all the ingredients are softened, about 20 minutes. Remove from the heat and, working in batches, transfer the mole to the blender along with the remaining soaking liquid, and purée until smooth, at least 4 minutes.

Heat the oil in a 6-qt (6-L) saucepan over medium-high heat. Add the mole and cook, whisking constantly, until slightly thickened, about 5 minutes. Add the chocolate, sugar, and 1 teaspoon salt, and cook until the mixture is smooth and the flavors have melded, about 10 minutes. Spoon the mole over the chicken to serve, and sprinkle with sesame seeds.

COOK'S NOTE: Serve with Red Rice with Achiote (page 123), if you like.

Nothing says comfort quite like home-style enchiladas—lightly fried corn tortillas coated in mild red chile sauce and rolled around shredded chicken and cheese. This version is not baked, but is made with hot ingredients and goes straight from pan to plate in the true Mexican style, so the enchiladas don't get soggy.

red chile enchiladas

2 cups (500 ml) Red Chile Sauce (page 174)

1 cup (250 ml) safflower or canola oil

Fine sea salt

18 corn tortillas, preferably homemade (page 106)

1½ cups (9 oz/270 g) shredded cooked chicken

¾ cup (3 oz/90 g) crumbled cotija or feta cheese, plus more for serving

1 medium white onion, minced, plus sliced white onion rings, for serving

Chopped fresh cilantro, for serving

serves 6–8

Prepare the red chile sauce as directed, or if made in advance reheat in a 12-inch (30-cm) frying pan. Remove from the heat and keep warm.

Heat the oil in another 12-inch (30-cm) frying pan over medium-high heat. Working in batches, grasp the tortillas with tongs and fry in oil until pliable, 30 seconds each. Transfer the tortillas to the frying pan with the enchilada sauce and toss to coat, then place on a work surface. Divide the chicken, cheese, and minced onion among the tortillas and roll each tortilla around the chicken to form tight rolls.

To serve, transfer the enchiladas to individual plates, and sprinkle with more cheese, onion rings, and cilantro. Serve.

COOK'S NOTES: These enchiladas are also delicious made with green tomatillo sauce (page 174).

The taste of the Yucatán is the distinctive, earthy flavor of *pib-il*, made from a marinade of red achiote and the curious but essential bitter orange. While *pib* means "pit" in the Mayan language, you can easily duplicate the effect in a home oven with this marinade and a banana-leaf wrap.

pibil-style baked chicken

1 large chicken, about 4 lb (2 kg), skin on and cut into 4 pieces (2 leg-and-thigh pieces and 2 breast halves)

2 tablespoons fresh bitter orange juice (see Cook's Note)

2 teaspoons achiote paste (page 182), diluted with 2 teaspoons water

2 cloves garlic, minced

Fine sea salt

9 pieces banana leaves, each approximately 16 inches (40 cm) square, defrosted if frozen

1 red onion, thinly sliced

2 tomatoes, thickly sliced

1 small güero chile, seeded and cut lengthwise into narrow strips

1 cup (100 g) Pickled Red Onions (page 139)

serves 4

Prick the chicken skin in several places with the tip of a sharp knife. In a small bowl, stir together the bitter orange juice, diluted achiote paste, garlic, and 1 teaspoon salt. Rub the chicken pieces all over with the mixture, then place in a sealable plastic bag, close, and refrigerate for at least 2 hours or up to overnight.

Preheat the oven to 375°F (190°C). Lay out 8 of the banana-leaf pieces, shiny side up. Tear the remaining leaf into 8 strips, ½ inch (12 mm) wide, to use as ties (they may need to be knotted together). Remove the chicken from the plastic bag, reserving the marinade. Layer half of the onion and tomato slices in the centers of 4 of the leaves. Top with a piece of the marinated chicken and a few strips of the chile. Top with the remaining onion and tomato slices. Drizzle on some of the marinade. Cover with another leaf, shiny side down, folding the edges together to seal. Tie each packet together with the ties.

Cut 4 pieces of aluminum foil, each about 12 by 14 inches (30 by 35 cm). Wrap each banana-leaf packet in a piece of foil and tightly crimp the edges until completely sealed. Place the packets on a baking sheet.

Bake the packets for 30 minutes, then turn over and cook for 20 minutes more. Remove 1 packet from the oven, open it, and use a knife to cut into the thickest part of the chicken; it should be opaque throughout. If it is not, rewrap and return to the oven for a few more minutes.

To serve, remove the foil and place each banana-leaf packet on an individual plate. Open the packets, top each portion with one-fourth of the pickled onions, and serve at once.

COOK'S NOTE: A citrus fruit that grows in parts of Mexico, the bitter orange is used widely in the cooking of the Yucatán peninsula. If you do not have access to the fruit, you can use a substitute made from other citrus juices: In a bowl, stir together 2 tablespoons fresh orange juice, 2 tablespoons fresh grapefruit juice, and 4 teaspoons fresh lime juice. Use at once, or cover and refrigerate for up to 2 days, although the taste diminishes.

Driving into the countryside with the family to eat pit-cooked *barbacoa* is a weekend tradition of long standing in Mexico. You won't have to dig a pit to enjoy this succulent braise cooked in a well-seasoned sauce of tomato and red chiles. Serve with a good sipping tequila.

short ribs barbacoa

4 pieces boneless beef short rib, pot roast cut, or chuck flat, each about 10 oz (300 g)

Fine sea salt and freshly ground black pepper

1 tablespoon vegetable oil or pork lard

½ rib celery, diced

½ yellow onion, diced

1 small carrot, peeled and diced

4 cloves garlic, split

2 bay leaves

1 teaspoon whole black peppercorns

½ teaspoon cumin seeds

1 whole clove

¼ teaspoon aniseeds

2 cups (500 ml) Red Chile Sauce (page 174) or store-bought enchilada sauce

8 cups (2 qt/2 L) chicken stock

TO SERVE

Corn tortillas, preferably homemade (page 106), warmed

1 avocado, pitted, peeled, and diced

½ white onion, diced and rinsed under cold water

Chopped fresh cilantro

serves 4

Preheat the oven to 350°F (180°C). Season the short ribs well on all sides with salt and pepper.

Heat a heavy frying pan over medium-high heat. Add the oil or lard and, when hot, sear the ribs until well browned on all sides, starting with the fat side down. Place in an ovenproof pot with a lid (such as a Dutch oven) just large enough to hold them in a single layer, almost touching.

Reduce the heat to medium. Cook the celery, onion, carrot, and garlic in the same frying pan, stirring occasionally, until light brown and softened. Add the bay leaves, peppercorns, cumin, clove, and aniseeds, and cook, stirring, for 1 minute. Add the red chile sauce to the pan, and cook the sauce until thickened, about 5 minutes.

Add 4 cups (1 qt/1 L) of the stock and bring to a simmer. Pour the sauce over the short ribs. The juices should come about halfway up the sides of the meat. Add a bit more chicken stock, if necessary. Set a piece of parchment paper, cut to fit the pot, directly on the short ribs. Wrap the pot tightly with foil and cover with the lid. Bake until the meat offers no resistance when a knife is inserted, 3–3½ hours.

Let the meat cool in the juices, loosely covered, for at least 1 hour, to allow the meat to reabsorb the flavors of the sauce. Transfer the meat to a platter and cover loosely. Strain the sauce into a bowl. Skim off as much fat as possible and pour the sauce into a flameproof baking dish. Add the remaining 4 cups (2 qt/2 L) stock to the casserole. Add the ribs and simmer gently for 10 minutes to reduce the sauce slightly. Turn the ribs a couple of times. Taste and adjust the seasoning.

Cut each short rib portion into three pieces and serve in small *cazuelas*, if you like, with plenty of sauce and warm tortillas on the side. Pass the avocado, onion, and cilantro in small bowls at the table.

Large, thin sheets of air-cured fresh beef called *cecina* are available for sale in Mexico's outdoor markets. Since this special cut is unavailable here, this recipe uses beef pounded out thinly and lightly "cured" overnight, then flash-grilled and generously smeared with brilliant green chimichurri sauce.

grilled beef cecina

1 lb (500 g) beef flap meat or boneless New York strip, 1 inch (2.5 cm) thick

1 teaspoon olive oil, plus more for greasing

Fine sea salt and coarsely ground black pepper

1 teaspoon ground California (dried Anaheim) chile

Mexican Chimichurri Salsa (page 131)

Sautéed Potatoes & Chiles (page 118)

¼ cup (1 oz/30 g) grated cotija or Romano cheese

serves 4

Carefully slice the meat horizontally into four 4-oz (100-g) portions. Place each slice between sheets of plastic and pound out as thinly as possible. Brush each piece with olive oil, 1 teaspoon salt, 1 teaspoon pepper, and ground California chile. Layer with plastic wrap and refrigerate for 24–48 hours.

About an hour before serving, make the chimichurri as directed on page 131. Next, prepare the potatoes and chiles according to the directions on page 118, and keep warm.

Warm four serving plates. Heat a heavy grill pan or iron pan over high heat. Brush the pan lightly with olive oil. Sear each piece of meat for 30 seconds on each side, and place on a warm plate. Sprinkle lightly with salt. Repeat with remaining meat. To serve, smear each portion with a spoonful of chimichurri, then top with a quarter of the potato mixture. Sprinkle with some of the cotija cheese, and serve immediately with the remaining chimichurri on the side.

The influence of Moorish Spain can be seen here in the blend of spices in the marinade, but the sauce is pure Mexican—a classic combination of pasilla chiles and tomatillos. Pasillas are dried ripe poblano chiles with a rich fruity flavor. Choose thick, best-quality lamb chops and grill them to bring out the flavor of the spices.

lamb chops with pasilla chile sauce

FOR THE LAMB

½ cup (125 ml) olive oil

Juice of 1 lemon

1 tablespoon minced garlic

2 teaspoons ground cumin

2 teaspoons ancho chile powder

½ teaspoon red pepper flakes

Fine sea salt and freshly ground black pepper

2 sprigs fresh oregano, minced

6 sprigs fresh flat-leaf parsley, minced

12–18 thick-cut lamb chops, 4–6 oz each

FOR THE SAUCE

4 large dried pasilla chiles (about 2 oz), preferably imported from Mexico

2 medium tomatillos, husked and rinsed

¼ yellow onion, sliced

1 clove garlic, sliced

⅛ teaspoon dried oregano, preferably Mexican, rubbed

1 cup (250 ml) chicken stock, preferably homemade (page 173)

serves 4–6

To prepare the lamb, in a bowl, combine the olive oil, lemon juice, garlic, cumin, ancho powder, red pepper flakes, 2 teaspoons salt, a sprinkling of pepper, the oregano, and parsley to make a paste. Smear the paste evenly to coat all sides of the lamb chops. Marinate at room temperature for at least 1 hour, or in the refrigerator up to overnight.

To make the sauce, heat a heavy griddle over medium-high heat. Remove the stems from the chiles, then cut a slit up one side of each chile and remove the seeds. Open the chiles up flat. One at a time, press the chiles flat onto the hot griddle until blistered and light brown. Turn and repeat. Tear into small pieces and set aside.

In a 2-quart saucepan over medium-high heat, combine the tomatillos, onion, garlic, ½ teaspoon salt, and 1 cup (250 ml) water. Bring to a simmer and cook until the tomatillos are barely soft, about 7 minutes. Remove from the heat. Add the chiles to the saucepan and press down into the hot liquid. Let soak for 15 minutes.

Place the contents of the saucepan, including the cooking liquid, in a blender. Add the oregano and purée until the sauce is completely smooth, 2 minutes. Add ¾ cup (180 ml) of the chicken stock and pulse to combine. Strain the sauce through a coarse sieve or food mill to remove all particles of chile skin. Rinse out the blender with the remaining ¼ cup (50 ml) stock and add to the sauce. You will have about 2 cups (500 ml) sauce. (At this point, the sauce may be refrigerated and reheated just before serving.)

Preheat a gas grill or cast-iron grill pan on high heat, or position an oven rack 4–6 inches (10–15 cm) below the broiler and preheat on high. Cook the chops on both sides to the desired doneness, as measured with an instant-read thermometer (130°F/54°C for medium-rare). For smaller chops, the cooking time may be as brief as 2–3 minutes per side.

Serve the chops on warmed plates, passing the sauce in a separate bowl.

Pipián is a different kind of mole, made with fresh green herbs, chiles, and seeds. Essential to the sauce are green pumpkin seeds, which enhance the lovely color. Tart tomatillos in the sauce make it a perfect foil for the rich meatiness of the roast duck.

duck in a green pipián

2 ducks, each 5–6 lb (2.3–2.7 kg), skin intact, cut into 4 pieces (2 leg-and-thigh pieces and 2 breast halves)

Fine sea salt and freshly ground black pepper

1 tablespoon safflower or canola oil

FOR THE PIPIÁN

½ cup (65 g) sesame seeds

2 tablespoons safflower oil

1 cup (130 g) raw pumpkin seeds, plus 2 tablespoons

12 tomatillos, husked and rinsed

½ white onion, coarsely chopped

12 serrano chiles, coarsely chopped

8 cloves garlic, coarsely chopped

8 sprigs fresh epazote

7 cups (1.75 L) chicken stock, preferably homemade (page 173), or duck stock

Fine sea salt

Seasoned White Rice (page 177), for serving

serves 6–8

Trim off any excess fat from the duck pieces and season them with salt and pepper. Prick the skin with a sharp knife, being careful not to pierce the flesh. In a large, heavy frying pan, heat the safflower or canola oil over medium-high heat. Add the leg-and-thigh pieces, skin side down, and fry, without turning, stopping to drain off the rendered fat from time to time, until browned, 10–15 minutes. Transfer to a plate and repeat to brown the breasts. Return the duck pieces to the pan, reduce the heat to medium-low, cover tightly, and cook until the meat is tender, about 40 minutes.

To prepare the seeds for the pipián, in a large, dry frying pan, toast the sesame seeds over medium heat until they start to turn golden, about 2 minutes. Let cool and transfer to a blender. In the same pan, heat the oil over medium heat. Add the pumpkin seeds and toast, stirring constantly, until plump, 1–2 minutes; do not let brown. Using a slotted spoon, remove the seeds, reserving 2 tablespoons for garnish and adding the rest to the blender. Set aside the pan with the oil.

In a saucepan over medium heat, cover the tomatillos with water. Bring to a simmer and cook until soft, about 10 minutes. Drain and add to the blender. Add the onion, chiles, garlic, epazote, and 1½ cups (350 ml) of the stock and process until smooth, adding more stock if necessary. Pour through a medium-mesh sieve placed over a bowl.

Return the reserved frying pan with the oil to low heat and reheat the oil. Pour in the sauce and stir frequently for about 5 minutes. Gradually add 4½ cups (1.1 L) stock and continue cooking over very low heat until the sauce thickly covers the back of a wooden spoon, about 10 minutes. Season to taste with salt. Add the duck pieces and warm thoroughly in the sauce. Transfer the duck to individual plates. Ladle the sauce over the duck, garnish with the reserved pumpkin seeds, and serve with the rice alongside.

Rural Mexican cooks make good use of local game. The slightly earthy, tangy flavor of wild-caught rabbit is a natural match for this rich chile sauce, which would pair equally well with a farm-raised rabbit or chicken.

rabbit in chile sauce

¾ cup (75 g) thinly sliced white onion, plus ½ white onion, coarsely chopped

⅓ cup (75 ml) fresh lime juice

Fine sea salt

1 rabbit, 2½–3 lb (1.25–1.5 kg), cut into serving pieces

6 green onions, coarsely chopped

4 cloves garlic, 2 left unpeeled, 2 peeled

20 large dried guajillo chiles, seeded

6 dried ancho chiles, seeded

½ teaspoon cumin seeds, crushed

½ cup (125 ml) safflower oil

1½ cups (350 ml) chicken stock, preferably homemade (page 173)

serves 4

Mix together the sliced onion, lime juice, and a sprinkling of salt in a glass bowl. Let macerate for about 2 hours.

Rinse the rabbit pieces well. Place in a saucepan with the green onions, unpeeled garlic, and a sprinkling of salt. Add water to cover and simmer, covered, for 1½ hours. Lift out the rabbit; discard the cooking liquid.

Place the guajillo and ancho chiles in separate bowls. Add very hot water to cover and let soak until very soft, about 15 minutes. Drain the anchos and transfer to a blender. Add the chopped onion, peeled garlic, cumin, and ¾ cup (180 ml) water. Blend to form a slightly textured purée. Pour into a bowl. Pour 1¼ cups (300 ml) water into the blender and gradually add the guajillo chiles, blending after each addition until almost smooth. Press through a sieve into the ancho purée. In a heavy, deep frying pan, heat the oil over medium heat until smoking. Add the chile sauce and fry, stirring, for 5 minutes. Add the rabbit and stock and cook until the sauce is thick, about 15 minutes. Season with salt.

Divide the rabbit evenly among individual plates and top with the sauce. Crown with a tangle of pickled sliced onion.

beans, sides & salads

Salads are not traditionally a big part of Mexican cuisine, but I find that they are becoming more and more popular for lunch, with perhaps some tasty *antojitos* and a bowl of soup. Especially in the summer months, Mexican cooks like to combine tart tomatillos with tangy chiles chipotles in adobo. It is an ideal dish to start a meal.

summer salad of tomatillos

1 lb (500 g) tomatillos, husked, rinsed, and chopped into ½-inch (12-mm) pieces

½ white onion, finely chopped

3 tablespoons finely chopped fresh cilantro

FOR THE DRESSING

¼ cup (50 ml) extra-virgin olive oil

1 or 2 canned chipotle chiles in adobo, finely chopped

1 teaspoon brown sugar

Fine sea salt

1 cup (4 oz/100 g) crumbled cotija or feta cheese

Fried tortilla chips or strips, preferably homemade (Totopos, page 107)

serves 6

In a bowl, toss together the tomatillos, onion, and cilantro.

To make the dressing, pour the olive oil into a small bowl, add half of the chipotle chiles, the brown sugar, and salt to taste, and whisk vigorously until well blended. Taste and add more chile, if desired. Remember, the dressing will not taste as potent after it is mixed with the tomatillos.

Spoon on enough of the dressing to coat the tomatillos thoroughly. Arrange on a platter and sprinkle with the cheese. The *totopos* can be served around the salad or in a separate bowl.

Stands selling fruit salads, along with fresh-made juices, are found everywhere in Mexico. Fresh-squeezed lime and a dash of salty, spicy *chile con limon* bring out the fruits' sweetness. The salads often come with a crunchy topping of toasted nuts and grain and yogurt or thick cream. Here, I combine fruit with crunchy vegetables, as they do in Mexico.

ensalada de frutas

FOR THE TOPPING

½ cup (50 g) rolled oats (not quick-cooking)

1 tablespoon vegetable oil

1 tablespoon agave syrup

2 tablespoons pumpkin seeds

2 tablespoons sliced almonds

2 tablespoons pecan pieces

1 tablespoon chia seeds

1 tablespoon white sesame seeds

Any combination of 3 or 4 ripe fruits cut into 1-inch (2.5-cm) pieces: pineapple, Mexican papaya, mango, banana, honeydew, watermelon, or strawberries

Cucumber or jicama, cut into small pieces

Unsweetened coconut chips

Lime wedges

Chile con limon seasoning (see page 182)

Crema, preferably homemade (page 177), or yogurt (optional)

serves 4–6

Preheat the oven to 325°F (160°C).

Combine the oats with the oil and agave syrup and toss until thoroughly coated. Add the pumpkin seeds, almonds, pecans, and chia and sesame seeds and stir to combine. Spread out on a rimmed baking sheet and toast in the oven, stirring twice, until golden brown and crunchy dry, 20–25 minutes. The topping will continue to crisp up once it is out of the oven. You will have 1 cup (120 g).

Prepare three or four different fruits and either the cucumber or jicama. Arrange on a platter, then sprinkle with the topping and coconut chips. Offer lime wedges, shakers of *chile con limon,* and, if desired, *crema* or yogurt on the side.

COOK'S NOTE: Substitute uncooked hot six-grain cereal for the rolled oats.

Cut thick or paper-thin, plantains are a favorite snack in Mexican homes. Although fried twice (once to cook and soften, and once to ensure they are golden and crisp), the fritters are very easy to prepare—and quick to disappear! They can also be made ahead of time (after being flattened) and frozen for up to 3 months.

fried green plantains

2 green plantains

3 cups (700 ml) canola oil

Fine sea salt

serves 4–6

To peel the green plantains, slice the ends off with a knife and make a lengthwise cut from one end to the other of the plantain skin. Remove the rest of the skin from the plantain. Slice the plantain into chunks 1–1½ inches (2.5–4 cm) wide.

To precook the plantains, heat the oil in a sauté pan over medium-high heat until it reaches 325°F (160°C) on a deep-frying thermometer. Lower the heat to medium and add the plantain chunks to the oil. Deep-fry the chunks, 3–4 minutes. Remove the chunks with a slotted spoon and drain on paper towels.

You can use a wooden press to flatten the plantains or do it with a heavy pan. Place an opened plastic bag over your wooden press or on your counter, put each plantain chunk inside the bag, and smash it with the top of the wooden press or with a heavy frying pan; do this while the plantains are still warm.

To finish the plantains, reheat the oil in the pan over medium-high heat until it reaches 350°F (180°C). Add the plantain chunks and deep-fry until lightly golden, about 2 minutes more. Remove to paper towels to drain and sprinkle with salt. Serve right away.

Hearts of palm and avocado, two popular ingredients in Mexico, come together in this vibrant, fresh salad. Choose from a mix of greens, such as red or green butter lettuce, endive, arugula, or baby spinach, in any combination.

mixed greens with hearts of palm, red onion & avocado

2 tablespoons fresh lime juice

Fine sea salt and freshly ground black pepper

2 teaspoons extra-virgin olive oil

3 tablespoons minced fresh cilantro, plus 1 cup (30 g) lightly packed whole leaves

6–8 cups mixed baby greens

2 avocados

1 can (14 oz/400 g) hearts of palm, drained

½ red onion, thinly sliced

serves 6

In a small bowl, whisk together the lime juice, ½ teaspoon salt, ¼ teaspoon pepper, the olive oil, and 1 tablespoon of the minced cilantro to make a dressing.

In a large bowl, toss the greens with the 1 cup (1 oz/30 g) cilantro leaves. Drizzle the dressing over the greens and toss to coat evenly.

Cut the avocados in half lengthwise and remove the pits. Working with one half at a time and using a paring knife, cut parallel lines in the avocado flesh, cutting just down to the peel. Use a large spoon to scoop the avocado slices into a bowl.

Rinse the hearts of palm and pat dry with paper towels. Cut each heart of palm crosswise into ½-inch (12-mm) slices.

To serve, divide the dressed greens among individual plates and top each serving with some of the sliced avocado, hearts of palm, and onion. Serve right away.

Good tortillas are available at most markets, but a *great* tortilla must be handmade and eaten fresh. Fortunately, it takes only a little practice with masa to develop a feel for handling and cooking the fresh dough.

corn tortillas

1 lb (450 g) freshly prepared tortilla masa or 1¾ cups (7 oz/200 g) masa harina for tortillas

Fine sea salt

1¼ cups (300 ml) plus 2 tablespoons warm water, if using masa harina

makes about 10 tortillas

If using fresh masa, put it in a bowl and knead with 1 teaspoon salt, adding a little warm water, if needed, to make a soft dough. If using masa harina, put in a bowl, add the warm water, and mix with your hands. Allow the dough to rest for 5 minutes, then add 1 teaspoon salt and knead for 1 minute. Shape into golf ball–sized balls, then cover with a damp kitchen towel or plastic wrap. Use a tortilla press to flatten the masa into thin disks (see page 178).

Heat a large griddle, cast-iron frying pan, or *comal* over medium heat. Slide the tortilla off your hand—do not flip it—onto the hot griddle. Cook until the underside is freckled, about 30 seconds. Flip over and cook for another 20–30 seconds, then flip back to the first side for just a second. Transfer to a plate. As the tortillas are cooked, stack them on a plate and cover with a kitchen towel to keep warm.

COOK'S NOTE: To reheat tortillas, wrap stacks of 5 tortillas each in aluminum foil and warm in a 275°F (140°C) oven for 5–10 minutes. To reheat fewer than 5 tortillas, put them back in the pan and reheat for several seconds on each side.

In Mexico, yesterday's tortillas are always put to good use—in enchiladas (page 88), as chilaquiles (page 70), or in tortilla soup (page 42). Or, you can always fry them crisp to make chips, which are called *totopos*, and tostadas.

totopos & tostadas

8 thin corn tortillas, 4–6 inches (10–15 cm) in diameter

Corn or peanut oil for frying

Fine sea salt (optional)

makes 8 tostadas or 3 cups (90 g) *totopos*

For *totopos*—chips, strips, or squares—stack the tortillas in 2 equal piles. Cut each pile into 4–6 triangular wedges, strips ¼ inch (6 mm) wide by 1 inch (2.5 cm) long, or small squares. Leave whole for tostadas. Spread in a single layer, cover with a heavy kitchen towel or wire rack to prevent curling, and let dry for at least several hours.

In a heavy frying pan, heat 1 inch (2.5 cm) oil over medium-high heat to 375°F (190°C) on a deep-frying thermometer. (If you don't have a thermometer, dip the edge of a tortilla into the oil; it should sizzle immediately and vigorously.)

Line a plate with paper towels. For tostadas, add the whole tortillas one at a time and lift out as soon as their color deepens. Drain on the paper towels. To make *totopos,* add the smaller pieces a few at a time and fry, tossing them, until light gold. Do not let them darken, or they will be bitter. Lift out and drain as for tostadas. Salt the *totopos,* if you like, while still hot.

Cover with a dry kitchen towel and keep warm for up to 30 minutes in a 200°F (90°C) oven. Store for up to 1 day, in an airtight plastic bag at room temperature. Recrisp, if necessary, for a few minutes in a 200°F (90°C) oven.

Dried fava beans, or *habas*, are used to make soups or fillings for stuffed items. This unique salad combines the cooked beans with a light, mildly spicy dressing inspired by *aguachile*, a style of ceviche popular in Baja California. The creamy *habas* contrast wonderfully against the fresh flavors of lime and herbs, ripe tomatoes, and crunchy red onion.

fava beans with citrus-herb sauce

8 oz (250 g) dried unshelled fava beans (about 1 cup)

Fine sea salt and freshly ground black pepper

¼ white onion

2 bay leaves

FOR THE SAUCE

¼ cup fresh lime juice

1 tablespoon minced fresh flat-leaf parsley

1 tablespoon minced fresh cilantro

1½ teaspoons sugar

¼ teaspoon dried oregano, preferably Mexican

1 small güero chile, seeded and minced (about 2 tablespoons), or ½ small serrano chile, seeded and minced (about 2 teaspoons)

½ cup (125 ml) olive oil

FOR SERVING

2 large, ripe tomatoes, thickly sliced

½ red onion, thinly sliced

serves 4–6

Pick over the beans and discard any misshapen beans or stones, then rinse under running cold water. In a large bowl, combine 4 cups (1 qt/1 L) cold water and 1 teaspoon salt and stir to dissolve the salt. Add the beans and soak for at least 4 hours or up to overnight.

Drain the beans in a colander and rinse well. In a large saucepan, combine the beans, onion, bay leaves, and 6 cups (1½ qt/1.5 L) cold water and bring to a boil over medium heat. Reduce the heat to medium-low and simmer until the beans are tender but not cracked, about 20 minutes. Drain thoroughly and transfer to a bowl. Discard the bay leaves.

To make the sauce, in a bowl, whisk together the lime juice, parsley, cilantro, sugar, oregano, chile, ½ teaspoon salt, and ½ teaspoon pepper. Add the olive oil in a thin stream, whisking constantly, until smooth and emulsified.

Pour the sauce over the beans and stir gently to avoid breaking up the beans. Let stand at room temperature to allow the flavors to blend, at least 20 minutes or until ready to serve.

To serve, divide the beans evenly among individual plates. Arrange the tomato and onion slices alongside and serve right away.

The blend of Mexican, Caribbean, and African elements in these simple beans makes them a true culinary treasure. Any other beans or legumes may be used instead of the black-eyed peas, and substitute soy chorizo to create an outstanding vegan dish.

black-eyed peas with chorizo

½ lb (250 g) dried black-eyed peas (about 1 cup/8 oz)

½ lb (250 g) fresh pork or beef chorizo, crumbled

Olive oil

1 large yellow onion, thinly sliced

¼ cup (1 oz/30 g) minced green onions, white and tender green parts

2 tomatoes, peeled and diced

½ serrano chile, seeded and minced

2 cloves garlic, minced

½ teaspoon achiote paste (page 182)

½ teaspoon ground cumin

Fine sea salt and freshly ground black pepper

5 sprigs fresh cilantro, plus cilantro leaves for serving

serves 4–6

Pick over the peas and discard any misshapen peas or stones. Rinse the peas under running cold water and drain. Place in a large bowl with cold water to cover generously and soak overnight.

Heat a frying pan over medium-high heat. Add the chorizo to the pan and cook, stirring as needed, until well browned. Using a slotted spoon, transfer the chorizo to paper towels and set aside, reserving the rendered fat in the pan.

Add olive oil as needed to the pan with the rendered fat to make 3 tablespoons total fat. (If you prefer, you can discard the rendered fat and use all olive oil.) Warm the fat over medium heat, then add the yellow and green onions and cook until translucent, about 5 minutes. Add the tomatoes, serrano, garlic, achiote, cumin, ½ teaspoon salt, and ½ teaspoon pepper and stir to mix well. Reduce the heat to medium low, cover, and cook, stirring occasionally, until the vegetables are tender, about 20 minutes.

Meanwhile, fill a wide pot three-fourths full of water and bring to a boil. Drain the peas in a colander and rinse well. Add the peas to the pot, reduce the heat, and simmer until very tender, about 30 minutes. Add 1 teaspoon salt and the cilantro sprigs and simmer to allow the flavors to blend, about 5 minutes. Drain the peas in a colander and remove the cilantro.

When ready to serve, spoon the peas onto a platter, top with the tomato stew and chorizo, and garnish with the cilantro leaves.

When the summertime grill is fired up, make this side dish with luscious beefsteak tomatoes. Topped with the brilliant green, garlicky chimichurri, they are the perfect accompaniment to grilled meats. The tomatoes can be served warm in whole pieces, as in this recipe, or chopped to create a flavorful salsa.

grilled tomatoes with mexican chimichurri sauce

2 tablespoons olive oil, plus more for greasing

1 tablespoon fresh lime juice

1 teaspoon dried oregano, preferably Mexican

Fine sea salt and freshly ground black pepper

3 large, ripe but firm tomatoes, halved

Mexican Chimichurri Salsa (page 131)

serves 4–6

Build a fire in a charcoal grill for direct grilling over high heat, or preheat a gas grill to high. Generously oil the grill rack and position it 2–4 inches (5–10 cm) above the coals.

In a bowl, whisk together the olive oil, lime juice, oregano, 1 teaspoon salt, and ½ teaspoon pepper and let stand at room temperature to marry the flavors, about 10 minutes. Add the tomato halves to the bowl and turn to coat thoroughly with the olive-oil mixture.

Brush the cut sides of the tomatoes with the chimichurri and arrange cut sides down on the grill rack directly over the hot coals. Grill until nicely marked, about 5 minutes. Baste the tops with the chimichurri. Using tongs, turn the tomatoes and grill on the other side until warmed through and nicely grill marked but still holding together and not mushy, about 5 minutes longer. Serve right away.

The combination of crunchy jicama, sweet citrus, and creamy avocado is especially popular during warmer weather, but can be enjoyed year-round. I love this version with tart pink grapefruit, a honey dressing, and a little dash of chile. It makes the perfect accompaniment to Carnitas Tacos (page 24) or Veracruz-Style Red Snapper (page 82).

jicama, grapefruit & avocado salad

2 small jicamas (about 1 lb/500 g total weight)

1 ruby red grapefruit

1 large avocado

FOR THE DRESSING

2 tablespoons fresh lime juice

1 tablespoon fresh orange juice

2 teaspoons honey

Pinch of cayenne pepper

Fine sea salt

¼ cup (15 g) fresh cilantro leaves

serves 4–6

Cut each jicama in half and, using a vegetable peeler or a sharp knife, remove the peel. Place the jicama halves cut side down on a cutting board, and cutting lengthwise, cut ¼-inch (6-mm) slices off the jicama. Stack the slices in piles of 3 or 4 and cut each stack crosswise into ¼-inch (6-mm) matchsticks. If some of the matchsticks seem too long, cut them in half. Place the matchsticks in a serving bowl.

Cut the ends off the grapefruit to expose the flesh and stand it upright on a cutting board. Following the curve of the fruit, cut away all the peel and the bitter white pith. Continue in this fashion, working your way around the fruit. Working over a bowl, make a cut on both sides of each segment to free it from the membrane, letting the segment and juice drop into the bowl below. Reserve 2 tablespoons of the grapefruit juice for the dressing.

Cut the avocado in half lengthwise and remove the pit. Using a paring knife, score each avocado half by cutting parallel lines just down to the peel, then turn it 90 degrees and cut another set of parallel lines perpendicular to the first ones. Scoop the avocado squares into the bowl with the jicama and grapefruit.

To make the dressing, in a small bowl, stir together the reserved grapefruit juice, the lime juice, orange juice, honey, cayenne, and salt to taste. Mix well to dissolve the honey completely. Pour about half of the dressing over the salad and toss gently. Taste, add more dressing if necessary, and adjust the seasoning.

Transfer the salad to a serving platter or individual bowls or plates, garnish with the cilantro leaves, and serve right away.

This is my favorite way to cook brown beans such as pintos. The resulting whole beans taste creamy and rich with pork and beef flavors and shredded meats; the hint of spicy chipotles in adobo adds a smoky undertone. It's easy to imagine a big pot of these simmering over a cook fire out on the range, under the stars.

frijoles charro

FOR THE BEANS

1 lb (500 g) dried pinto or other brown beans (about 2⅓ cups)

Fine sea salt and freshly ground black pepper

1 teaspoon red pepper flakes

1 teaspoon oregano, preferably Mexican

½ medium onion, diced

2 large cloves garlic, split

4 oz (100 g) pork skin or fat back

8 oz (250 g) fatty bone-in pork chop or smoked pork chop

2 beef marrow bones (12–16 oz/350–500 g) or 1 whole beef oxtail (8 oz/225 g)

FOR THE FRYING

2 tablespoons vegetable oil or pork fat

¼ onion, finely diced (½ cup)

2 large cloves garlic, minced

2 canned chipotle chiles in adobo, chopped

12 fresh large epazote leaves, chopped

1½ cups diced tomato (one 14.5-oz/400-g can)

makes 10 cups (1.8 kg)

To prepare the beans, pick over the beans and discard any misshapen beans or stones, then rinse. In a large pot, combine the beans, 10 cups (2½ qt/2.5 L) water, 1 tablespoon salt, 1 teaspoon black pepper, red pepper flakes, oregano, onion, garlic, pork, and beef. Bring to a simmer and cook, covered, at a low simmer until the beans are very tender, 2½–3 hours. Remove and discard all bones, break up the meat, and add back to the pot.

To fry the beans, in a 4-qt (4-L) pot, heat the oil over medium heat. Sauté the diced onion, garlic, chopped chipotles in adobo, 1 teaspoon black pepper, and epazote leaves until softened and fragrant, but not browned. Add the tomatoes and the cooked beans with all their liquid. Simmer, stirring often, until thickened slightly, 1 hour.

COOK'S NOTES: Vegetarians may substitute ½ cup (50 g) soy bacon bits for the meats, and vegetable oil for the lard. Beer lovers may swap 1 bottle of beer for 1½ cups (350 ml) of water. Pork skin or fatback can be diced small and fried until golden brown, and added back to the pot. Carnivores can also crumble a few *chicharrones* (pork rinds) on top for a crunchy contrast. The cooked beans freeze well.

The everyday bean of the Yucatán is the small black turtle bean. The beans are cooked with plenty of epazote, garlic, and beer, then mashed smooth or chunky, as you prefer. I love using these in huevos rancheros or in burritos. Vegans can omit the pork and substitute smoky-flavored soy bacon bits for great depth of flavor.

yucatecan refried black beans

FOR THE BEANS

2 tablespoons vegetable oil

¼ white onion, diced

2 large cloves garlic, minced

2 teaspoons ground cumin

1 teaspoon dried oregano

1 teaspoon red pepper flakes

Fine sea salt and freshly ground black pepper

1 can Mexican beer

1 lb (500 g) dried black beans (about 2⅓ cups), rinsed and picked over

1 smoked pork hock

6 large fresh epazote leaves

FOR THE FRYING

2 tablespoons vegetable oil or pork lard

1 tablespoon minced serrano chile

¼ white onion, minced

2 large cloves garlic, minced

1 teaspoon dried oregano

10 large epazote leaves, chopped

Grated queso añejo, cotija, or Romano cheese, for serving

Pico de gallo salsa, preferably homemade (page 129), for serving

makes 7 cups (1.7 kg)

To prepare the beans, in a deep 4-qt (4-L) pot with a lid, heat the oil over medium heat. Add the onion, garlic, cumin, oregano, red pepper flakes, and 1 teaspoon pepper. (Add soy bacon bits here, if you are using them instead of the pork hock.) Cook, stirring, until the spices are fragrant.

Add the beer, 8 cups (2 qt/2 L) water, the beans, pork hock, epazote leaves, and 1 teaspoon salt. Bring to a low simmer, cover, and cook until the beans are perfectly tender and falling apart, 2½–3 hours. Remove the pork hock. Shred the meat from the bone and set aside.

To fry the beans, in a deep 4-qt (4-L) pot with a lid, heat the oil over medium heat. Sauté the serrano, onion, garlic, oregano, and epazote until softened, but not browned. Add the cooked black beans and juices to the pot, a couple of cups at a time, mashing the beans as much as possible with a potato masher, and cooking down before adding more. (They will splatter as they cook, so keep a splatter guard or the lid handy.) Small amounts of water or beer can be added as the beans are fried, to keep them loose. The beans will thicken more after cooking.

Serve very hot, sprinkled with grated cheese and a teaspoon of *pico de gallo* on each serving.

Rajas, Spanish for "strips," are slices of roasted chiles and are often combined with grilled or sautéed onions and garlic. Serve the ragout alongside grilled or roasted meats, spoon it over rice, or toss it with pasta.

three-bean ragout with rajas

½ cup (3½ oz/100 g) dried black beans

½ cup (3½ oz/100 g) dried kidney beans

½ cup (3½ oz/100 g) dried pinto beans

6 tablespoons (90 ml) extra-virgin olive oil

3 tablespoons white wine vinegar

½ teaspoon dried oregano, preferably Mexican

Pinch of sugar

Fine sea salt and freshly ground black pepper

3 tablespoons olive oil

1 small white onion, slivered

1 large clove garlic, coarsely chopped

2 poblano chiles roasted, peeled, and seeded (page 178), then cut into narrow strips 1 inch (2.5 cm) long

1 large red bell pepper, roasted, peeled, seeded, and cut into narrow strips 1 inch (2.5 cm) long

1 large yellow bell pepper, roasted, peeled, seeded, and cut into narrow strips 1 inch (2.5 cm) long

serves 8

Keeping the black, kidney, and pinto beans separate, pick them over, discarding any misshapen beans or stones. Rinse well, then soak in water to cover for at least 4 hours or up to overnight. Drain the beans and place each variety in a separate small saucepan. Add water to cover generously, bring to a boil, reduce the heat to a simmer, and cook until tender, about 1 hour.

In a large bowl, whisk together the extra-virgin olive oil, vinegar, oregano, sugar, and salt and pepper to taste to make a dressing. When the beans are ready, drain them and add to the dressing while the beans are still warm. Toss well. Set the beans aside, stirring them every so often while you finish the recipe.

In a large frying pan, heat the olive oil over medium-high heat. Add the onion and sauté until softened, about 3 minutes. Add the garlic and cook for 1 minute longer. Add the chile strips, bell pepper strips, and beans, reduce the heat to low, and cook, stirring, until all the ingredients are heated through, just a few minutes. Season the ragout with salt and pepper and transfer to a warmed bowl. Serve immediately.

This combination of charred poblano chiles with creamy potatoes, onions, cheese, and garlic is one of my favorites. It isn't as rich as it may appear; the sour cream and cheese very lightly coat the other ingredients and let the flavors shine through. It makes a sensational taco filling.

sautéed potatoes & chiles

1 lb (500 g) white fingerlings or other small potatoes, cooked and thinly sliced

2 tablespoons olive oil

¼ white onion, thinly sliced

2 cloves garlic, thinly sliced

2 poblano chiles, roasted, peeled, and seeded (page 178), then cut into narrow strips

Fine sea salt

½ cup (125 ml) *crema*, preferably homemade (page 177), or sour cream

¼ cup (1 oz/30 g) grated cotija cheese

serves 4

Put the potatoes in a 4-qt (4-L) saucepan and cover with water by 1 inch (2.5 cm); bring to a boil over high heat and cook until just tender, about 20 minutes. Drain and set aside.

Heat 1 tablespoon of the olive oil in a 12-inch (30-cm) frying pan over medium-high heat. Add the onion and garlic and cook, stirring, until soft, about 5 minutes. Add the chile strips and cook, stirring, until heated through, about 2 minutes. Remove from the pan and keep warm.

Add the remaining 1 tablespoon olive oil to the pan, increase the heat to medium-high, and add the sliced potatoes in a single layer. Allow to brown before turning, then season with ¼ teaspoon salt. Stir in the chile and onion mixture, *crema,* and serve warm, sprinkled with the cheese.

Sweet potatoes, native to South America, were once a significant part of the pre-Hispanic diet but now are more apt to be found made into candies cooked in *pilocillo* syrup, such as the famous *camotes* of Puebla, or steam-baked and sold by vendors for a tasty and filling morning or evening snack.

spiced baked sweet potatoes

4 sweet potatoes, well scrubbed

¾ cup (160 g) firmly packed brown sugar or chopped *piloncillo* sugar (page 186)

⅓ cup (75 ml) fresh lime juice

⅓ cup (75 ml) fresh orange juice

1½ teaspoons ground cinnamon

½ teaspoon ground allspice

4 tablespoons (60 g) unsalted butter (optional)

Fine sea salt and freshly ground pepper

serves 4

Preheat the oven to 400°F (200°C).

Poke a few holes in the top of each sweet potato and place the potatoes on a baking sheet. Bake until soft to the touch, about 45 minutes. The timing will depend on the size of the sweet potatoes.

Just before the sweet potatoes are ready, in a saucepan, stir together the brown sugar or *piloncillo,* lime and orange juices, cinnamon, and allspice. Place over low heat and cook, stirring, until the sugar dissolves and the mixture is syrupy, about 3 minutes.

When the sweet potatoes are done, remove them from the oven and let cool slightly so they can be handled. Slit vertically and lightly mash the flesh inside with a fork, adding an equal amount of the butter to each one, if desired.

Place the potatoes in a serving dish. Pour an equal amount of the syrup into each opening, season with salt and pepper, and mash the syrup into the flesh, letting it puddle in the dish. Serve immediately.

Aztec corn goddess Teotzintle rules the Mexican table. Corn in some form appears at almost every meal. Fresh corn, called *elote*, is a popular street food. It may be served simply boiled, roasted, or grilled over charcoal and slathered with spices, fresh lime, and cheese. There is no better way to celebrate the season.

mexican corn on the cob three ways

FOR A SPICY TOPPING

2 teaspoons chili powder

1 teaspoon ground cumin

¼ teaspoon fine sea salt

¼ teaspoon cayenne pepper

FOR PARMESAN & LIME TOPPING

5 tablespoons (1½ oz/ 40 g) finely grated Parmesan cheese

Grated zest of 2 limes

¼ teaspoon fine sea salt

FOR COTIJA & CILANTRO TOPPING

1¼ cups (5 oz/150 g) finely crumbled cotija or feta cheese

½ cup (15 g) loosely packed fresh cilantro leaves, finely chopped

Pinch of fine sea salt

4 ears of corn

4 tablespoons unsalted butter, softened

8 tablespoons mayonnaise

serves 4

Choose your desired topping(s) and stir the ingredients together in a small bowl.

For grilled corn, build a medium-hot fire in a charcoal grill or preheat a gas grill to medium-high. Keeping the stalk intact, remove all but a few of the outer husks from the ears of corn. Arrange the corn on the grate directly over the heat and grill, using tongs to rotate every couple of minutes, until blackened in spots all over, about 8 minutes. Transfer the corn to a platter and let cool briefly, then remove the remaining husks and silks (alternatively, pull back the remaining husks and use a husk to tie in place).

For boiled corn, bring a large pot of lightly salted water to a boil. Remove the husks and silks from the corn and carefully drop the corn into the boiling water. Cook until fork-tender, about 8 minutes. Using tongs, transfer to a colander and let drain, then transfer to a platter and let sit for about 10 seconds to allow any water clinging to the ears to evaporate.

Once you have grilled or boiled the corn, immediately brush each ear of corn with 1 tablespoon butter and then with 2 tablespoons mayonnaise. Sprinkle with your topping and serve right away.

This rice's emerald green color comes from a purée of highly nutritious chiles and herbs. Toasting the rice and chiles together concentrates the flavors. The recipe can be doubled, and leftover rice keeps well in the freezer.

arroz verde

Packed ½ cup (20 g) fresh cilantro leaves (about half a small bunch), plus 1 tablespoon chopped, for serving

1 poblano chile, roasted, peeled, and seeded (page 178)

½ jalapeño chile, stemmed

1 large clove garlic, peeled but left whole

¼ white onion

Fine sea salt

1 tablespoon vegetable oil

1 cup (200 g) white or brown rice

serves 4

In a blender, combine the cilantro, poblano, jalapeño, garlic, onion, 1 teaspoon salt, and ¼ cup (50 ml) water. Pulse and scrape down the sides frequently to achieve a very smooth, bright green purée.

In a saucepan with a lid, heat the oil over medium heat. Add the rice and cook and stir until the rice has absorbed the oil and is tinged with gold, 5 minutes. Add the cilantro purée and cook and stir until the purée has thickened and become aromatic, 1 minute. Add 1¾ cups (425 ml) water, stir once to settle, and bring to a gentle boil. Cover and turn the heat to low. Cook until all the liquid is absorbed, 15–20 minutes for white rice or 30–40 minutes for brown rice. Do not stir.

When the rice is dry, turn off the heat and let stand, covered, for 5 minutes. Fluff gently with a fork. Stir the chopped cilantro into the cooked rice, and serve.

This garlicky orange-red rice looks like the familiar Mexican red rice, but achiote paste gives it a subtle spark of flavor. The deep orange paste, popular in the kitchens of the Yucatán peninsula, is made from the hard seeds of the tropical annatto tree.

red rice with achiote

2 medium-large, ripe tomatoes, chopped, or 1 can (14.5 oz/400 g) diced tomatoes, drained

½ cup (60 g) chopped white onion

2 cloves garlic, chopped

1 tablespoon achiote paste (page 182)

1 green bell pepper

⅓ cup (75 ml) safflower or canola oil

2 cups (400 g) medium- or long-grain white rice

3 cups (700 ml) chicken stock, preferably homemade (page 173)

5 sprigs fresh flat-leaf parsley, chopped, plus a few sprigs for garnish

Fine sea salt

serves 8–10

In a blender, purée the tomatoes, onion, and garlic. Add the achiote paste and blend until well mixed. Pass the mixture through a sieve.

Char the bell pepper on all sides directly in a gas flame, or under a broiler, until the skin is blackened and blistered. Peel, seed, and cut into short, narrow strips.

In a heavy saucepan, heat the oil over medium heat. Add the rice and cook, stirring, until it starts to turn light gold, about 5 minutes. Stir in the tomato purée and fry, scraping the pan bottom occasionally, until the purée is absorbed into the rice, about 3 minutes. Stir in the stock and add the bell pepper, parsley sprigs, and 1 teaspoon salt, or to taste. Reduce the heat to medium-low, cover, and cook the rice for 25 minutes. When the rice is almost cooked through, remove the pan from the heat and leave covered for 10 minutes.

Toss the rice with a fork, then spoon into a warmed bowl, garnish with parsley sprigs, and serve.

salsas & condiments

Guacamole is usually kept simple, with just a squeeze of fresh lime juice and a little salt. Equally popular are festive, seasonally inspired guacamoles like this fall specialty of central Mexico, which is sparked with crunchy onion, spicy chile, and a sprinkling of fresh herbs and studded with crunchy, tart pomegranate seeds.

guacamole with mango & pomegranate

3 ripe avocados

2 teaspoons fresh lime juice

Fine sea salt

¼ small white onion, finely diced

1 small serrano chile, seeded and minced

3 sprigs fresh cilantro, stemmed and chopped

2 tablespoons diced mango

2 tablespoons pomegranate seeds

½ small plum tomato, seeded and finely diced (about 2 tablespoons)

FOR SERVING

1 small jicama, peeled and cut into sticks

Fried tortilla chips or strips, preferably homemade (Totopos, page 107)

serves 4

Cut the avocados in half and remove the pits. Scoop the flesh into a bowl or *molcajete* (mortar). Using a fork, a potato masher, or a pestle, mash the avocado with the lime juice and ½ teaspoon salt until the guacamole is smooth but still has a little texture and some chunks. Stir in the onion, serrano, and cilantro. Taste and adjust the seasoning.

Spoon the guacamole into a serving bowl or leave it in the *molcajete*. Scatter the mango, pomegranate seeds, and tomato on top. Serve right away with the jicama sticks and tortilla chips for dipping.

COOK'S NOTE: Pretty red pomegranate seeds and mango are used here, but any tart-sweet fruit, such as pineapple and strawberries, work just as well. Or, try crumbling 1 tablespoon salty cotija or goat cheese, or 1 tablespoon toasted pumpkin seeds, over the top with the fruit and tomato.

This very simple rustic sauce is served with *barbacoa* of lamb.
It is traditionally thinned with *pulque*, a mildly alcoholic fermented
beverage made from the sap of the maguey, a type of agave.

drunken pasilla chile salsa

5 pasilla chiles, lightly toasted (page 178)

3 cloves garlic, coarsely chopped

1 thin slice white onion, coarsely chopped

¾ cup (6 fl oz/180 ml) fresh orange juice

¼ cup (2 fl oz/60 ml) beer or tequila blanco

½ teaspoon sea salt

makes 1½ cups (375 ml)

In a bowl, combine the toasted chiles with very hot water to cover and let soak until soft and pliable, about 15 minutes. Drain the chiles and tear into pieces. Place in a blender or food processor along with the garlic, onion, orange juice, and beer or tequila. Purée until smooth.

Pour the salsa into a small serving bowl and season with the salt. The salsa can be made up to a week in advance, as it improves with age. Store, covered, in the refrigerator.

COOK'S NOTE: Try with tacos of grilled steak.

If you're pressed for time but want to create a full-flavored
Mexican meal, this simple, creamy salsa combines the
best of tomato salsa and guacamole in one bowl.

tomato-avocado salsa

2 large ripe tomatoes

1 ripe avocado

2 green onions

¼ cup (60 ml) olive oil

¼ cup (10 g) minced cilantro

¼ cup (60 ml) lime juice

1 teaspoon dried oregano, preferably Mexican

Sea salt and black pepper

serves 4–6

Seed and dice the tomatoes. Pit, peel, and dice the avocado. Mince the white and pale green parts of the green onions. In a nonreactive bowl, whisk together the olive oil, green onions, cilantro, lime juice, oregano, 2 teaspoons salt, and ½ teaspoon pepper and stir to mix well. Add the tomatoes and avocado and stir gently to coat with the dressing. Refrigerate until ready to serve.

The smoke-dried jalapeño, known as the chipotle chile, adds a distinctive wood-fire flavor to this simple tomato table salsa from the Puebla region.

chipotle chile salsa

3 dried chipotle chiles or canned chipotle chiles in adobo

2 cloves garlic, unpeeled, roasted (page 178)

2 ripe tomatoes, about 12 oz (350 g) total weight, roasted (page 178)

Fine sea salt

makes 1 cup (250 ml)

If using dried chiles, simmer them in salted water to cover until softened, 10–15 minutes. Drain, reserving the liquid, and place the chiles in a blender or food processor along with about ¼ cup (50 ml) of the liquid. If using canned chiles, scrape off some of the adobo sauce and put the chiles in a blender or food processor.

Peel the charred skin from the garlic and add the garlic to the blender along with the tomatoes. Process very briefly. The mixture should be thick and slightly chunky.

Pour into a bowl, season to taste with salt, cover, and let the flavors meld for 20–30 minutes before serving.

Fresh and colorful, *salsa fresca* adds a welcome burst of flavor to just about everything. For a more robust salsa flavored with chile and lime, make *pico de gallo* (see variation below).

salsa fresca

2 plum tomatoes

¼ white onion, finely diced

2 tablespoons finely chopped fresh cilantro

Fine sea salt

makes ¾ cup (180 ml)

Seed the tomatoes and dice finely. Place in a bowl and add the onion, cilantro, and ½ teaspoon salt. Stir to mix well, taste, and adjust the seasoning. Serve right away, or store in an airtight container in the refrigerator for up to 3 days.

PICO DE GALLO SALSA VARIATION: Add 1 serrano or jalapeño chile, minced with its seeds, and fresh lime juice to taste to the salsa fresca.

Chimichurri is as popular in Mexico as it is in South America, where it originated. This lovely bright green sauce has a fresh taste that goes particularly well with simple grilled meat dishes.

mexican chimichurri salsa

2 large cloves garlic

Fine sea salt and coarsely ground black pepper

1 tablespoon fresh lime juice

3 tablespoons extra-virgin olive oil

¼ teaspoon red pepper flakes

¼ bunch fresh flat-leaf parsley, minced

¼ bunch fresh cilantro, minced

makes ⅔ cup (160 ml)

In a small bowl or a mortar, crush and mash the garlic into a paste with ¼ teaspoon salt, using a fork or pestle. Stir in the lime juice, oil, red pepper flakes, ½ teaspoon pepper, the parsley, and cilantro.

COOK'S NOTE: To store chimichurri, like pesto, place in a small airtight container and cover with a thin layer of olive oil to slow discoloration. Refrigerate for up to a week.

Parsley is widely associated with chimichurri sauce, but the most traditional version doesn't use it—in fact, it doesn't use fresh herbs at all. Let sit before using so the flavors can marry.

traditional chimichurri sauce

Fresh sea salt and freshly ground black pepper

4 cloves garlic, minced

1 tablespoon dried oregano

1 tablespoon dried rosemary, minced

1 tablespoon dried thyme

2 bay leaves, finely crumbled

1 teaspoon chile powder

½ cup (125 ml) white vinegar

2 tablespoons olive oil

makes 1 cup (250 ml)

In a saucepan, bring 1 cup (250 ml) water to a boil over high heat. Add 1½ teaspoons salt and stir to dissolve. Meanwhile, in a heatproof glass jar with a tight-fitting lid, combine the garlic, oregano, rosemary, thyme, bay leaves, chile powder, and ¼ teaspoon pepper. Pour the hot salted water into the jar. Add the vinegar and olive oil, cover tightly, and store in a dark place for at least 4 hours, but ideally 1 week.

In the Yucatán peninsula, the habanero is the chile most often used in salsas. Charring deepens its distinctive sweet heat, and even the tomato tastes sweeter when roasted. This warm salsa is used to give a zing to virtually any type of bean dish.

roasted habanero & tomato salsa

1 small green bell pepper

4 ripe tomatoes, roasted (page 178)

3 tablespoons safflower or canola oil

1 white onion, chopped

1 habanero chile, roasted (page 178) and slit partially on all 4 sides

Fine sea salt

makes 2 cups (500 ml)

Char the bell pepper on all sides directly in a gas flame, or under a broiler, until the skin is blackened and blistered. Peel, seed, and tear into small pieces.

In a blender or food processor, combine the bell pepper and the tomatoes with all their juices and coarsely purée. In a saucepan, heat the oil over medium heat. Add the onion and sauté until golden, about 3 minutes. Stir in the tomato mixture and fry until the sauce changes color, about 3 minutes. Add the habanero and simmer over medium-low heat for about 15 minutes to blend the flavors.

Just before serving, remove and discard the habanero and stir in 1 teaspoon salt, or to taste. Serve hot. (The salsa will keep for 4 days, covered, in the refrigerator. Reheat before serving.)

The cooking of the Yucatán is unique to Mexico, reflecting the region's traditional ingredients and Mayan heritage. This lovely, thick salsa adds creaminess (without cream) and a real kick of long-lasting heat from the habanero chile.

pumpkin seed salsa

1¼ cups (160 g) raw, unhulled pumpkin seeds

2 plum tomatoes, cored

1 habanero or Scotch bonnet chile, stemmed

3 tablespoons finely chopped fresh cilantro

3 tablespoons finely chopped fresh chives

Fine sea salt

makes 1½ cups (350 ml)

Heat an 8-inch (20-cm) frying pan over medium-high heat. Add the pumpkin seeds and cook, swirling the pan often, until lightly toasted, about 3 minutes. Transfer to a food processor and process until smooth, about 45 seconds; set aside.

Return the frying pan to the heat and add the tomatoes and chile; cook, turning as needed, until charred all over, about 5 minutes for the chile, 7 minutes for the tomatoes. Transfer to the food processor with the pumpkin seeds, along with the cilantro, chives, and salt to taste, and pulse until smooth.

Transfer to a bowl and cover with plastic wrap. Store in the refrigerator until 30 minutes before serving. Serve at room temperature.

COOK'S NOTE: This salsa is terrific with any kind of seafood or vegetable dish. A serrano or jalapeño may be substituted for less heat. If you like thinner salsa, add up to 1 cup (250 ml) vegetable stock or water to the mixture in the food processor.

This sprightly mixture of mango, cucumber, lime, and orange is a wonderful warm-weather accompaniment to grilled chicken or fish dishes.

mango & cucumber salsa

2 mangoes

1 orange

½ cucumber, peeled, seeded, and cut into small dice

Juice of 1 lime

2 serrano chiles, finely chopped

Fine sea salt

makes 3 cups (700 ml)

Peel, pit, and dice the mangoes, and place in a nonmetallic bowl.

Remove the zest from half of the orange in long, thin strips, cut into ½-inch (12-mm) pieces, and add to the bowl. Cut the ends off the orange to expose the flesh and cut away all the peel and the bitter white pith. Cut along either side of each segment to free it, then dice the segments. Remove any seeds and add the diced orange to the bowl.

Add the cucumber, lime juice, and serranos. Toss well, season to taste with salt, and toss again, then serve right away or store in an airtight container in the refrigerator for up to 1 day.

This perfectly balanced salsa combines crunchiness, sweet-acid pineapple, and just a hint of spiciness. It is outstanding with pork *carnitas* or on a beer-battered fish taco or other fried food.

pineapple-jicama salsa

½ pineapple

1 small jalapeño

1 cup (130 g) peeled and diced jicama

½ cup (15 g) loosely packed fresh cilantro leaves, chopped

⅓ cup (50 g) finely chopped red onion

2 tablespoons olive oil

1 tablespoon fresh lime juice

Fine sea salt and freshly ground black pepper

makes 3½ cups (650 g)

Peel, core, and dice the pineapple. Seed and mince the jalapeño. In a glass or ceramic bowl, gently toss together the pineapple, jalapeño, jicama, cilantro, onion, olive oil, and lime juice. Season to taste with salt and pepper. Let the salsa stand at room temperature for about 15 minutes, stirring once or twice. Serve right away or store in an airtight container in the refrigerator for up to 1 day.

WATERMELON AND JALAPEÑO VARIATION: In a glass or ceramic bowl, gently toss together 2½ cups (380 g) small cubes seedless watermelon, the cilantro, onion, jalapeño, olive oil, and the zest and juice of 1 lime. Season with salt and pepper and serve right away.

In northern Mexico, pan-roasted chiles and onions are typically served alongside grilled steaks, meat tacos, or *guisados* (stews). The key to great flavor is patiently getting some char on the onions and chiles, which brings out the sweetness of the chile as a foil to the heat. In Baja California, these are often finished with a squeeze of lime or lemon and a dash of soy sauce.

blistered serrano chiles with caramelized onions

12 serrano chiles, halved lengthwise (see Cook's Note)

2 tablespoons safflower or canola oil

1 medium white onion, thinly sliced lengthwise

Fine sea salt

¼ cup (50 ml) chicken stock or water

Juice of 1 lime

serves 4

Heat a 12–inch (30-cm) frying pan over high heat. Add the chiles and cook, stirring occasionally, until charred all over, about 14 minutes. Add the oil and onion, season to taste with salt, and cook, stirring occasionally, until the onion is soft and slightly charred, about 8 minutes.

Add the stock or water and lime juice to the frying pan and stir to scrape up any browned bits from the pan bottom. Simmer until the liquid is half evaporated, about 2 minutes. Remove from the heat, and serve warm.

COOK'S NOTE: For a less spicy dish, remove the seeds and ribs from the chiles before cooking them.

Crunchy cabbage is a popular year-round garnish for tacos, soups, and stews. This sweet-tart slaw is a colorful and nutritious addition to most anything. The slaw can be dressed well ahead of time and will still hold its crunch. You can also try other shredded vegetables such as Brussels sprouts, sweet bell peppers, kale, or broccoli.

tangy cabbage & carrot coleslaw

2 tablespoons olive oil

Zest and juice of 1 lime

1 teaspoon honey

1 clove garlic, minced

1 small jalapeño chile, seeded and minced

Fine sea salt and freshly ground black pepper

1 cup (90 g) shredded green cabbage

1 cup (90 g) shredded red cabbage

1 large carrot, shredded (about ¾ cup/120 g)

makes 2½ cups (300 g)

In a large bowl, stir together the olive oil, lime zest and juice, honey, garlic, and jalapeño. Season well with salt and pepper.

Stir in the cabbages and carrot and toss until well coated with the dressing. Let the slaw stand at room temperature for about 10 minutes, stir again, and serve right away.

CREAMY CILANTRO SLAW VARIATION: In a large bowl, stir together 3 tablespoons mayonnaise, 1 teaspoon distilled white vinegar, the garlic, and the jalapeño and season with salt and pepper. Add the cabbages, carrot, and ½ cup (30 g) loosely packed fresh chopped cilantro. Gently toss and serve right away.

Pickled vegetables are a fixture at taco stands and market stalls, acting as both palate cleanser and condiment. The carrots will absorb capsaicin and may become even hotter than the chiles.

pickled jalapeños & carrots

1½ cups (350 ml) distilled white vinegar

¼ cup (50 g) sugar

Fine sea salt

1 bay leaf

5 peppercorns

3 jalapeño chiles, sliced

1 large carrot, peeled and sliced on the diagonal

½ red onion, sliced

makes 3 cups (560 g)

Combine the vinegar, sugar, ¼ teaspoon salt, bay leaf, and peppercorns in a heavy saucepan over medium heat and cook, stirring once or twice, until the sugar and salt dissolve, about 2 minutes.

Add the jalapeños, carrot, and onion and reduce the heat to low. Cook, stirring occasionally, for 10–15 minutes. Using a slotted spoon, transfer the pickles to a serving bowl and let cool. Serve right away, or store in an airtight container in the refrigerator, with enough pickling liquid to cover, for up to 2 weeks.

Pickled onions accompany practically every meal on the Yucatán peninsula, and for good reason. They contribute the perfect tang of vinegar and crunch of onion—without too much raw onion bite.

pickled red onions

1 habanero chile

2 small red onions, thinly sliced

Boiling water

⅓ cup (75 ml) fresh lime juice

2 cloves garlic, slightly smashed

Fine sea salt and freshly ground black pepper

⅛ teaspoon dried oregano, preferably Mexican

makes 2 cups (200 g)

Pan-roast the chile (see page 178). Set aside to cool.

Place the onion slices in a heatproof bowl and add boiling water to cover. Let soak for 2–3 minutes. Drain well, transfer to a small bowl, and toss with the lime juice, garlic, 1 teaspoon salt, ¼ teaspoon pepper, and the oregano. Tuck the chile under the onions and let marinate at room temperature for 1 hour, stirring occasionally.

Before serving, retrieve the chile and place it on top of the onion slices. Serve right away, or store in an airtight container in the refrigerator for up to 2 weeks.

Here's a unique salsa that is garlicky, sweet, and smoky all at once. It is great with roasted vegetables, chicken, and fish or shrimp. Try making it with orange or yellow bell pepper in season.

smoky red pepper salsa

1 large red bell pepper

3 plum tomatoes

2 cloves garlic

1 tablespoon vegetable oil

¼ white onion, diced

2 teaspoons ground cumin

1 tablespoon smoked Spanish paprika

Fine sea salt

6 sprigs fresh cilantro, stemmed and minced

makes 2 cups (500 ml)

Char the bell pepper on all sides directly in a gas flame, or under a broiler, until the skin is blackened and blistered. Peel, seed, and tear into smaller pieces.

Line a small heavy sauté pan (cast iron is ideal) with a piece of foil and heat over high heat. Roast the tomatoes and one garlic clove until soft and blackened in spots, and set aside with the bell pepper.

In a medium frying pan, heat the oil over medium heat. Cook the onion until it begins to brown and caramelize. Add the tomatoes and peppers, cumin, and paprika and cook until the pan is dry. Add ½ cup (125 ml) water and ½ teaspoon salt and simmer on low heat until the onions are tender. Place in a food processor along with the remaining raw garlic clove and pulse until fairly smooth. Stir in the cilantro, taste, and adjust the seasoning.

If using this spicy salsa for Grilled Chiles Rellenos Stuffed with Shrimp Rice (page 78), don't overdo the chipotles—the poblano chiles and the rice are mildly spicy as well.

salsa diabla

4 plum or pear tomatoes

½ small white onion

2 cloves garlic

1–2 tablespoons canned chipotles in adobo

1 tablespoon olive oil

Fine sea salt

2 tablespoons butter

2 tablespoons roughly chopped cilantro

makes 2½ cups (600 ml)

Roughly chop the tomatoes, onion, and garlic, add to a blender with chipotles to taste, and purée.

Set a 1-quart saucepan over medium-high heat. Add the olive oil and, when hot, pour in the puréed tomato mixture (it will splatter, so be careful). Cook, stirring, until the purée is thickened and bubbling. Add 1½ cups (350 ml) water and salt to taste, reduce the heat to medium, and bring to a simmer.

Just before serving, whisk in the butter and add the cilantro. You may want to thin the sauce slightly with more water. Taste and adjust the seasoning and serve hot.

This salsa balances heat and sweetness, which makes it ideal to accompany almost anything. Try to source true Mexican pasilla chiles—their deep color and flavor make the salsa memorable.

pasilla & árbol chile salsa

4 árbol chiles

2 dried pasilla chiles, preferably imported from Mexico

2 cloves garlic, unpeeled

6 ripe plum tomatoes, roughly chopped

Juice of ½ lime

Fine sea salt

makes 2 cups (500 ml)

Toast the chiles (page 178), then seed. Roast the garlic (page 178), then peel. In a saucepan over medium heat, combine the chiles with water to cover and bring to a simmer. Cook for 5 minutes, remove from the heat, and let soak for about 10 minutes. The chiles should be very soft.

Put the garlic, tomatoes, and lime juice in a blender or food processor and blend only until broken up. Drain the chiles, tear into small pieces, and add to the tomato mixture. Add ½ teaspoon salt and process to a slightly rough-textured consistency. If the mixture is too thick, add a few tablespoons of water. Transfer to a bowl and serve. (The salsa will keep for 1 day, covered, in the refrigerator.)

If you are fortunate enough to have a mortar made of volcanic rock *(molcajete)*, this sweet but tart salsa can be made in it. Serve with chips, tacos, or grilled meats, fish, or chicken.

spicy avocado salsa

8 oz (250 g) tomatillos (10–12)

½ white onion

3 serrano chiles

¾ cup (45 g) chopped fresh cilantro, plus whole leaves for garnish

1 teaspoon brown sugar

2 avocados, pitted

Fine sea salt

makes 3 cups (700 ml)

Husk, rinse, and roughly chop the tomatillos. Cut the white onion into small chunks. Roughly chop the serranos. In a blender, combine the chiles, onion, and ½ cup (125 ml) water. Process until partially smooth. Add the tomatillos, chopped cilantro, and brown sugar and blend until the mixture is roughly textured.

Scoop the avocado flesh into a bowl and coarsely mash with a fork. It should be chunky. Stir in the chile mixture and season with salt. Lightly garnish with cilantro leaves and serve. (The salsa will keep for 3 hours, covered, in the refrigerator.)

Roasting the tomatoes for a salsa adds a welcome smoky flavor and concentrates their sweet flavor, improving even pale winter tomatoes. In season, try making this salsa with half tomatillos and half tomatoes.

fire-roasted tomato salsa

1 lb (500 g) ripe plum tomatoes

1 jalapeño chile

3 cloves garlic, unpeeled

½ white onion, quartered

2 teaspoons olive oil

⅓ cup (10 g) loosely packed fresh cilantro leaves, chopped

1 teaspoon red wine vinegar

Fine sea salt

makes 1¾ cups (400 g)

Position an oven rack 6 inches (15 cm) below the broiler and preheat on high. Line a baking sheet with aluminum foil.

Cut the tomatoes in half lengthwise and arrange cut side down on the prepared pan. Place the jalapeño, garlic, and onion on the pan so everything is in a single, uncrowded layer. Drizzle with the olive oil. Broil, turning the vegetables once and rotating the pan as needed, until the vegetables are charred all over, about 5 minutes per side. Remove from the oven and let cool.

When cool enough to handle, seed the jalapeño and peel the garlic. Combine the tomatoes, jalapeño, garlic, onion, and cilantro in a blender or food processor. Process until the salsa is well combined and there are no large chunks left, but the salsa still has plenty of texture. Add the vinegar and pulse to combine. Season to taste with salt. Serve right away or store in an airtight container in the refrigerator for up to 1 week.

Tart tomatillos are an essential ingredient in salsas, available year-round throughout Mexico and often easier to come by than tomatoes, which are seasonal. Roasting the tomatillos and onions slightly tempers their flavors, while a whole serrano adds a welcome kick of heat.

salsa verde

1 lb (500 g) tomatillos, husked and rinsed

1 serrano chile

3 cloves garlic, unpeeled

½ white onion, finely chopped

½ cup (15 g) loosely packed fresh cilantro leaves

Fine sea salt

makes 2½ cups (600 g)

Position an oven rack 6 inches (15 cm) below the broiler and preheat on high. Line a baking sheet with aluminum foil.

Cut the tomatillos in half and arrange them cut side down on the prepared pan. Place the serrano and garlic on the pan so everything is in a single, uncrowded layer. Broil, turning everything once and rotating the pan as needed, until the vegetables are charred all over, 4–5 minutes per side. Be sure not to overcook the tomatillos, or they will fall apart and lose much of their flavor. Remove from the oven and let cool.

When cool enough to handle, remove the stem from the chile and peel the garlic. Combine the tomatillos, serrano, garlic, onion, cilantro, and ¼ teaspoon salt in a blender or food processor and process to a coarse purée. Taste and adjust the seasoning, then serve right away or store in an airtight container in the refrigerator for up to 1 week.

sweets

Known in Spanish as *tuna*, the fruit of the prickly pear cactus has juicy flesh and a flavor reminiscent of watermelon. If you cannot find the fresh fruits, cans or bottles of the juice can be bought in Latin markets or online.

fresh fruits in prickly pear syrup

FOR THE SYRUP

2½ lb (1.25 kg) prickly pears (14–16 fruits) or 2 cups (500 ml) unsweetened prickly pear juice

1 cup (200 g) sugar

1 bunch fresh mint

1 stick cinnamon, preferably Mexican *canela*

1 vanilla bean, split lengthwise

FOR THE FRUIT

1 large, ripe mango, peeled, pitted, and cut into ½-inch (12-mm) dice

1 small, ripe pineapple, peeled, halved lengthwise, cored, and cut into ½-inch (12-mm) dice

6 large strawberries, hulled and quartered lengthwise

1 cup (150 g) blueberries

1 cup (150 g) blackberries

1 cup (120 g) raspberries

6 sprigs fresh mint, for garnish (optional)

serves 6

To make the syrup, if using fresh prickly pears, working with one fruit at a time and using the tip of a sharp knife, scrape off the thorny nodes. Trim off the ends of the fruit, make a lengthwise slit through the skin, and peel off and discard. Repeat with the remaining fruits. Cut the fruits into large pieces, transfer to a food processor, and purée, 10–12 seconds. Strain through a medium-mesh sieve. You should have 2 cups (500 ml).

In a saucepan, combine the prickly pear purée or juice, ½ cup (125 ml) water, the sugar, mint, and cinnamon stick. Scrape the seeds from the vanilla bean into the pan, then add the pod halves. Bring to a boil over medium-high heat, stirring to dissolve the sugar. Reduce the heat to medium-low and simmer, uncovered, for 20 minutes. Taste and make sure the flavors are balanced. Strain through a fine-mesh sieve.

To prepare the fruit, place the mango in a bowl with the pineapple and mix gently to combine. Place a spoonful of this fruit mixture in each of 6 small glass bowls or martini glasses. Divide the strawberries, blueberries, blackberries, and raspberries among the bowls. Ladle the syrup over the fruits, garnish with mint sprigs, if using, and serve.

Paletas (ice pops) are made fresh daily at small *paleterias* across the country. The frozen treats are often wild combinations of savory and sweet, spicy and herbal, incorporating both fruits and vegetables. These simple-to-make pops balance sweet mango with an interesting edge of mild chile.

mango-chile ice pops

1 cup (250 ml) store-bought mango juice or nectar

¼ cup (50 g) sugar

2 teaspoons fresh lemon juice

1 teaspoon ancho chile powder

1 large mango, peeled, pitted, and diced

makes 8 ice pops

In a 1-qt (1-L) saucepan, heat the mango juice, sugar, lemon juice, and ½ cup (125 ml) water over medium-high heat, stirring until the sugar dissolves. Transfer the mixture to a bowl and refrigerate until chilled.

Stir the ancho powder and diced mango into the chilled mixture and pour into eight 3-oz (90-ml) ice-pop molds. Insert an ice-pop stick into each mold and freeze until the pops are solid, about 3 hours more.

To release ice pops from their molds, run the bottoms of the molds briefly under cold water.

COOK'S NOTE: If mango isn't available, substitute papaya, passion fruit, or even blackberries and their juices in these ice pops.

This simple recipe combines voluptuously sweet mango with the slightly tart flavor of unaged white tequila. The flambéing burns off most of the alcohol and leaves behind the haunting agave flavor of the spirit. Keep a pan lid handy in case you need to smother the flames.

mangoes flambéed with tequila

3 tablespoons unsalted butter, cut into small pieces, plus more for greasing

6 ripe mangoes, about 3 lb (1.5 kg) total weight

3 tablespoons dark brown sugar

Finely shredded zest of 1 lime

Finely shredded zest of ½ orange

1 tablespoon fresh lime juice

1 tablespoon fresh orange juice

¼ cup (50 ml) tequila blanco

1 qt (1 L) coconut or French vanilla ice cream

½ cup (1½ oz/40 g) shredded unsweetened coconut, toasted (see Cook's Note)

serves 6

Preheat the oven to 400°F (200°C). Lightly grease an attractive shallow baking dish measuring about 9 x 13 inches (23 x 33 cm).

Peel and pit each mango, cutting the flesh into slices. Arrange the slices in a slightly overlapping fashion in the prepared dish. Sprinkle with the brown sugar and dot with the butter. Scatter the lime and orange zests over the top, then drizzle with the lime and orange juices.

Bake, uncovered, until the mango slices begin to brown, about 20 minutes. Though best served immediately, the mangoes can be kept warm for about 30 minutes.

When ready to serve, sprinkle the tequila over the mangoes and carefully ignite with a long match. Jiggle the pan for a moment until the flames die out, then divide among individual plates. Add a scoop of ice cream to each plate and garnish with a sprinkle of toasted coconut.

COOK'S NOTE: To toast shredded coconut, preheat the oven to 350°F (180°C). Evenly spread the coconut in a thin layer in a baking dish or on a sheet pan and toast, stirring frequently, until golden brown, 7–10 minutes.

This variation of French toast, served for dessert, was brought to Mexico by the Spaniards who followed in the wake of the conquest. In Spain and throughout Europe, the humble but delicious dish is known as "poor knights." True Mexican cinnamon elevates it to a new level.

caballeros pobres

¾ cup (150 g) sugar

Two 3-inch (7.5-cm) sticks cinnamon, preferably Mexican *canela*

6 whole cloves

6 allspice berries

½ teaspoon aniseeds

1 cup (6 oz/180 g) raisins

1 cup (3 oz/90 g) sliced almonds

4 large eggs, separated

Fine sea salt

2 tablespoons unsalted butter

1 teaspoon safflower or canola oil

12 baguette slices, each ¾ inch (2 cm) thick, crusts removed

serves 6

Put the sugar in a 1-qt (1-L) saucepan and stir in 1½ cups (350 ml) water. Add the cinnamon sticks, cloves, allspice, and aniseeds. Bring to a simmer over medium heat, stirring gently, until the sugar is dissolved. Cover and continue to simmer for 2 minutes longer. Strain, add the raisins and almonds to the syrup, and let cool.

In a bowl, whisk together the egg whites and a pinch of salt until fluffy. Lightly whisk the egg yolks in a small bowl just until blended, then fold into the whites.

In a frying pan, melt the butter with the oil over low heat. Raise the heat to medium and, working in batches, dip the bread slices in the egg batter, then place in the pan. Fry, turning once, until slightly crisp, 5–6 minutes total. Transfer to paper towels to drain. Arrange the slices in a serving dish and pour the syrup over the top. Let stand for 15–20 minutes. Serve warm or at room temperature.

Sopaipillas appear in many forms throughout Mexico (and, indeed, Central and South America) under many names. Some quick-bread versions, albeit with less airy results, are made with baking powder or baking soda in place of yeast, and some use richer batters with cooked *zapallo* (pumpkin) folded in. This classic recipe is perfect with black coffee any time of day.

sopaipillas

FOR THE DOUGH

1 teaspoon active dry yeast

1 teaspoon granulated sugar

¼ cup (50 ml) warm water (105°–115°F/40°–45°C)

2½ cups (310 g) all-purpose flour, or as needed, plus more for dusting

Fine sea salt

¾ cup (180 ml) whole milk

2 tablespoons unsalted butter

Safflower or canola oil, for greasing and deep-frying

FOR SERVING

Confectioners' sugar

Honey

makes 24 *sopaipillas*

In a small bowl, dissolve the yeast and sugar in the warm water and let stand until foamy, about 5 minutes.

In a food processor, combine 2 cups (250 g) of the flour and ½ teaspoon salt and pulse to mix, about 5 seconds. Add the yeast mixture, the milk, and the butter and pulse to mix, about 20 seconds. Add the remaining ½ cup (60 g) flour and process just until a moist dough forms and pulls away from the sides of the bowl, about 10 seconds. If the dough seems too sticky, add 2 tablespoons flour and pulse until soft but not sticky, about 10 seconds.

Lightly oil a large bowl. Place the dough in the bowl and turn to coat with the oil. Cover with a clean kitchen towel and let stand in a warm, dark place until doubled in bulk, about 1 hour.

When the dough has risen, in a deep saucepan, heat 3 inches (7.5 cm) oil over medium-high heat to 375°F (190°C) on a deep-frying thermometer. Line one large baking sheet with parchment or waxed paper and one baking sheet with paper towels.

Turn the dough out onto a lightly floured work surface and roll out to a thickness of about ¼ inch (6 mm). Using a small, sharp knife or a round cookie cutter, cut out 24 squares or rounds. Place on the parchment-lined baking sheet.

Slip a few *sopaipillas* into the hot oil and fry, using tongs to turn as needed, until lightly golden on all sides, 2–3 minutes total. Transfer to the paper towel–lined baking sheet to drain. Repeat to fry the remaining *sopaipillas*. Divide the *sopaipillas* among individual plates and dust with confectioners' sugar. Serve right away, with honey on the side for drizzling.

I am lucky to have a spot in my garden where enough figs ripen once a year to make this traditional recipe from northern Mexico, where figs are bountiful. Intensely sweet tree-ripened figs are often difficult to find in supermarkets. Look for them at their seasonal peak, in summer, at farmers' markets.

baked figs with goat cheese

4 tablespoons (60 g) unsalted butter, cut into small cubes, plus more for greasing

12 ripe Mission figs

¼ cup (60 g) firmly packed dark brown sugar

⅓ cup (40 g) walnut halves

¾ cup (3 oz/90 g) crumbled fresh goat cheese

serves 4

Preheat the oven to 350°F (180°C). Grease a shallow baking dish in which the figs will fit snugly once they are cut.

Snip the stems from the figs and quarter the figs from the stem end down to, but not quite through, the bottoms. Spread the figs open and place cut side up in the prepared baking dish. Sprinkle evenly with the brown sugar, scatter the walnuts on top, and dot with the butter.

Cover and bake until the figs are heated through, about 20 minutes. Spoon some of the crumbled goat cheese onto each fig and, if desired, lightly toast the cheese in a broiler or very hot oven for just a few minutes.

Serve the figs warm or at room temperature on individual plates with some of the syrup that forms during baking spooned over the tops.

Along with candy, Mexican *dulcerias* offer an unusual variety of candied and preserved vegetables, such as winter squash and various types of cactus. One of the most common and delicious is *camotes* (orange sweet potatoes) cooked in a heavy syrup of *piloncillo* sugar and spices. It can be served as a sweet or side dish.

sweet potatoes stewed in syrup

1 lb (450 g) *piloncillo* sugar (page 186), roughly chopped, or 2 cups (425 g) firmly packed brown sugar

1 cup (250 ml) fresh orange juice

2 lb (1 kg) sweet potatoes, peeled and cut into 1½-inch (4-cm) chunks

3-inch (7.5-cm) stick cinnamon, preferably Mexican *canela*

1-inch (2.5-cm) piece fresh ginger, peeled and finely chopped

Zest of 1 orange (with no white pith), roughly chopped

2 teaspoons fresh lime juice

Fine sea salt

serves 6

Heat the *piloncillo,* orange juice, and ½ cup (125 ml) water in a 6-qt (6-L) saucepan over medium-high heat, stirring often, until dissolved, 10 minutes. Add the sweet potatoes, cinnamon, ginger, and orange zest; reduce the heat to medium-low, and cook, covered and stirring occasionally, until the potatoes are tender, about 30 minutes.

Using a slotted spoon, transfer the sweet potatoes to a large serving dish and continue cooking the liquid until reduced to a syrupy consistency, about 30 minutes more.

Stir in the lime juice and a pinch of salt and pour the syrup over the sweet potatoes. Serve warm or at room temperature.

COOK'S NOTE: Butternut or acorn squash, pumpkin, and even carrots can substitute for or supplement the sweet potatoes in this recipe.

When a rich, fancy dessert is just not the thing, this rustic, moist corn cake is usually perfect with an after-dinner coffee. The sweet cake is often paired with a salty accompaniment, such as *crema* (page 177) or *queso fresco* (try any salty fresh cheese).

pan de elote

8 tablespoons (120 g) unsalted butter, at room temperature, plus 2 tablespoons

½ cup (100 g) sugar, plus more for sprinkling (optional)

1 cup (6 oz/180 g) fresh corn kernels

4 large eggs, at room temperature

1 tablespoon all-purpose flour

1 teaspoon baking powder

Fine sea salt

1 tablespoon corn oil

serves 8

Preheat the oven to 350°F (180°C).

In a bowl, using an electric mixer, beat together the 8 tablespoons (120 g) butter and the sugar until creamy. Put the corn kernels in a food processor and process until ground, with some texture remaining. Add the ground corn to the butter mixture and beat until well mixed. Beat in the eggs one at a time, beating well after each addition. Add the flour, baking powder, and 1 teaspoon salt and beat until just combined.

Put the remaining 2 tablespoons butter and the oil in a 9-inch (23-cm) ovenproof frying pan or quiche dish and heat in the oven until the butter is melted. Add the creamed corn mixture and bake until set and a toothpick inserted into the middle comes out clean, about 20 minutes. There should be no liquid visible when the pan is shaken or tilted. Remove from the oven and sprinkle with sugar, if desired.

Cut the cake into wedges and serve directly from the pan.

Classic vanilla-scented flan is simple and delicious, but this version, touched with coffee liqueur and dark rum, brings a hint of the exotic flavors of Mexico's Caribbean coast. It makes a luxurious finale to an elegant meal.

kahlúa & rum flan

8 cups (½ gal/2 L) whole milk

1⅔ cups (325 g) sugar

2-inch (5-cm) stick cinnamon, preferably Mexican *canela*

6 large eggs, plus 4 large egg yolks

2 tablespoons Kahlúa or other coffee liqueur

1 tablespoon dark rum

1 teaspoon pure vanilla extract

Ground cinnamon, for serving (optional)

serves 6–8

In a large saucepan over medium-low heat, bring the milk, 1 cup (200 g) of the sugar, and the cinnamon to a boil, stirring to dissolve the sugar. Reduce the heat to low. Simmer uncovered, stirring frequently, until the milk is reduced by half, about 45 minutes. (In order to judge accurately when the milk has reduced sufficiently, pour half of the milk into the pan before you add the remainder, to see where the final level should be.) Set aside to cool.

Place the remaining ⅔ cup (125 g) sugar with ¼ cup (50 ml) water in a small, heavy saucepan over medium-high heat and bring to a boil. Continue to boil without stirring until the syrup begins to color, about 15 minutes. Reduce the heat to a simmer, then swirl the pan until the syrup is a deep amber, about 1 minute. Immediately pour the caramel into individual custard cups or a 2½-qt (2.5-L) soufflé dish, tilting to distribute the caramel evenly over the bottom. Some of the syrup may run up the sides of the dish, but try to keep most of it on the bottom. Set aside.

Preheat the oven to 350°F (180°C). In a large bowl, beat the eggs, egg yolks, Kahlúa, rum, and vanilla until blended. Slowly beat in the milk mixture. Pour the mixture through a fine-mesh sieve into the prepared cups or dish. Place the cups or dish in a baking pan and pour in hot water to reach three-fourths up the side of the cups or dish. Cover loosely with aluminum foil.

Bake until just set and the tip of a knife inserted in the middle comes out clean, 30–40 minutes for individual cups and 40–50 minutes for the soufflé dish. Remove the baking pan from the oven and let the flan cool in the water. (The flan can be covered and refrigerated for up to 2 days.)

To unmold, run a knife around the edge of the mold(s) to loosen the custard. Invert a deep serving plate or individual plate over the top, and invert the flan and dish together. The flan should drop from the mold. If it resists unmolding, dip the mold(s) in hot water for just a few seconds, then invert. The flan should drop out easily. Sprinkle with ground cinnamon, if using, and serve at once.

Hot chocolate has its roots in an ancient grain-based drink, *atole*, once made exclusively for the pleasure of Aztec royalty. Today, sweet hot chocolate is a favorite street food, served accompanied with a paper bag of piping-hot, crispy deep-fried churros for dunking.

spiced hot chocolate with churros

FOR THE HOT CHOCOLATE

¼ cup (1 oz/30 g) masa harina

2 cups (500 ml) whole milk

1 disk (3 oz/90 g) Mexican chocolate, coarsely chopped

3 tablespoons crushed *piloncillo* sugar (page 186) or brown sugar

½ teaspoon ground cinnamon

1 teaspoon pure vanilla extract

¼ teaspoon aniseeds, toasted and crushed

FOR THE CHURROS

Salt

3 tablespoons granulated sugar

1 cup (120 g) all-purpose flour, sifted

2 large eggs, beaten

Safflower or canola oil for deep-frying

1 long strip lemon zest

1 tablespoon ground cinnamon

serves 4–6

To make the hot chocolate, in a saucepan, combine the masa harina and 2 cups (500 ml) water and cook over medium-low heat, whisking constantly, until the mixture thickens, about 3 minutes. Whisk in the milk. Add the chocolate and *piloncillo* sugar and stir until the chocolate melts and the sugar dissolves, about 3 minutes. Add the cinnamon, vanilla, and crushed aniseeds and simmer, stirring constantly, for about 2 minutes. Reduce the heat to very low to keep the hot chocolate hot; do not let boil.

To make the churros, in another saucepan, combine 1 cup (250 ml) water, 1 teaspoon salt, and 1 tablespoon of the granulated sugar. Bring to a boil over high heat, then remove from the heat and immediately add the flour, all at once. Beat with a wooden spoon until the dough is very smooth and pulls away from the sides of the pan, about 2 minutes. Let cool for 5 minutes, then beat in the eggs, about 1 tablespoon at a time. When all of the eggs are thoroughly incorporated, spoon the dough into a pastry bag fitted with a large star tip and twist the bag closed.

Pour 1 inch (2.5 cm) oil into a heavy frying pan and heat over medium heat to 350°F (180°C) on a deep-frying thermometer. Add the lemon zest and cook until browned, about 5 minutes. Remove and discard. Pipe several strips of dough, each 3–4 inches (7.5–10 cm) long, directly into the hot oil, being careful not to crowd the pan. Cut the dough strips free from the piping tip with a knife or scissors, dipping the tool in the oil before each cut. Fry the churros, turning as needed, until deep golden brown and very crisp, 3–5 minutes. Using a skimmer, slotted spoon, or tongs, transfer to paper towels to drain briefly, then place in a large bowl. Repeat to cook the remaining churros.

In a small bowl, stir together the cinnamon and the remaining 2 tablespoons granulated sugar. Add to the bowl with the warm churros and toss to coat evenly. Serve warm, with cups of the hot chocolate for sipping and dunking.

This is one of many Mexican desserts that owe a debt of gratitude to the Spanish culinary influence—or, more precisely, to the Moors, who originally introduced the almond to Spain. I like to spoon on a colorful raspberry sauce flavored with a splash of almondy amaretto.

almond ring

FOR THE CAKE

Oil or butter for greasing

5 large egg whites, at room temperature

Fine sea salt

¾ cup (150 g) granulated sugar

3 cups (15 oz/430 g) blanched almonds, finely ground

3 tablespoons unsalted butter, melted and cooled

¼ teaspoon almond extract

FOR THE RASPBERRY SAUCE

2 cups (240 g) fresh or thawed frozen raspberries

½ cup (100 g) superfine sugar

1 tablespoon fresh lemon juice

¼ cup (50 ml) amaretto liqueur

Confectioners' sugar for dusting (optional)

serves 8–10

Preheat the oven to 350°F (180°C). Lightly grease a 4-cup (1-L) ring mold or 6-cup (1.4-L) Bundt pan.

To make the cake, in a bowl, using an electric mixer, beat together the egg whites and a pinch of salt until soft peaks form. Gradually add the granulated sugar and continue to beat until stiff peaks form. Fold in the ground almonds, cooled melted butter, and almond extract. Gently pour the mixture into the prepared mold.

Bake the cake until it is golden and a toothpick inserted into the middle comes out clean, about 30 minutes. Let cool in the mold on a rack for 10 minutes, then run a knife blade around the edges to loosen the cake and turn out onto a serving plate. Let cool completely.

To make the sauce, set aside some whole berries. In a blender or food processor, purée the remaining berries until broken up. Add the superfine sugar, lemon juice, and amaretto and continue to process until smooth. Strain through a fine-mesh sieve.

Slice the almond ring and place the slices on individual plates. Top with the sauce, garnish with the reserved whole berries and, if desired, confectioners' sugar, and serve.

Tres leches is as rich as pudding and definitely *not* for the calorie conscious. This recipe tops the cake with a glossy meringue, but you can substitute whipped cream. For a stunning presentation, serve on a colorful platter garnished with fresh berries or with tropical fruits like starfruit, papaya, mango, and pineapple.

tres leches cake

FOR THE CAKE

½ cup (4 oz/120 g) vegetable shortening, plus more for greasing

2¼ cups (280 g) sifted all-purpose flour, plus more for dusting

1½ cups (300 g) sugar

2 large eggs

2 teaspoons baking powder

Fine sea salt

1 cup (250 ml) whole milk

1 teaspoon pure vanilla extract

FOR THE TRES LECHES SAUCE

1 can (14 oz/430 ml) sweetened condensed milk

1 can (12 oz/350 g) evaporated milk

1 cup (250 ml) heavy cream

2 tablespoons dark rum

1 teaspoon pure vanilla extract

Preheat the oven to 350°F (180°C). Line a 9 x 12–inch (23 x 30–cm) baking pan with aluminum foil and lightly grease the foil. Dust the foil-lined pan with flour and tap to shake out the excess.

In a bowl, using an electric mixer set on high speed, beat the shortening until fluffy. Add the sugar a little at a time, beating until fluffy between each addition. Reduce the speed to low and add the eggs one at a time, beating until fully incorporated after each addition and scraping down the sides of the bowl as needed, about 2 minutes total.

Sift the flour again with the baking powder and ½ teaspoon salt into a large bowl. In a small bowl, whisk together the milk and vanilla. Add one-third of the milk mixture to the shortening and beat until well mixed, then add one-third of the flour mixture. Repeat twice more, beating well after each addition. Scrape the batter into the prepared pan and bake until a small wooden skewer or cake tester inserted into the center of the cake comes out clean, about 35 minutes. Transfer to a wire rack and let cool in the pan for 10 minutes, then invert the cake onto a platter large enough to hold it and let cool completely. (Alternatively, you can finish the cake and serve it from the pan.)

To make the *tres leches* sauce, in a bowl, whisk together the condensed milk, evaporated milk, cream, rum, and vanilla.

When the cake has cooled completely, poke it all over with the tines of a fork, and spoon the sauce over the surface, a little at a time, allowing the cake to absorb the sauce before adding more. By the end, a little sauce may have pooled on the platter, but the cake should absorb almost all of it. Cover the cake with plastic wrap and refrigerate for about 1 hour.

FOR THE MERINGUE FROSTING

1 cup (8 oz/250 g) sugar

4 large egg whites, at room temperature

¼ teaspoon cream of tartar

serves 12

To make the meringue frosting, in a small, heavy saucepan, combine the sugar and ½ cup (125 ml) water and bring to a boil over medium-high heat, stirring to dissolve the sugar. Reduce the heat to medium-low and simmer, using a pastry brush dipped in cold water to wash down the sides of the pan as crystals form.

When the syrup comes to a boil, start beating the egg whites: in a clean metal bowl, combine the egg whites and cream of tartar and, using an electric mixer set on high speed, beat until stiff peaks form. While you are beating the eggs, continue to boil the sugar syrup until a candy thermometer registers 230°F (110°C), 10–12 minutes. Slowly add the boiling syrup in a thin stream to the egg whites while beating until all the syrup is incorporated. Continue beating until the meringue frosting is cooled and glossy. Cover and refrigerate until ready to use.

Spread the meringue frosting on the chilled cake, cover, and refrigerate again until well chilled, at least 3 hours and up to 8 hours. Serve chilled, cut into squares.

This little *torta* is like an over-the-top chocolate coconut macaroon. It's a decadent treat, (especially topped with the *nata*, thick unsweetened cream), but it is going to ring all your happy chimes. Cook in small ramekins, or use as a tart filling with a simple prebaked cookie or nut crust.

chocolate-coconut torta with nata

1 can (14 oz/400 g) coconut milk

1 cup (9 oz/250 g) best-quality semisweet chocolate, chopped into small pieces

1½ cups (350 ml) sweetened condensed milk

¼ teaspoon salt

4 large eggs plus 2 large egg yolks, at room temperature

½ teaspoon ground cinnamon

1 tablespoon dark rum

2 teaspoons vanilla extract

2 cups (6 oz/180 g) shredded sweetened coconut

Cooking spray

1 cup (250 ml) heavy whipping cream (see Cook's Note)

makes ten 6-oz (180-ml) ramekins, or one 8-inch (20-cm) tart

Heat the coconut milk and chocolate over low heat until the chocolate is melted. Scrape into a blender. Add the sweetened condensed milk, salt, eggs, egg yolks, cinnamon, rum, and vanilla. Blend on low speed until completely combined. Add the coconut and pulse until the coconut is broken up. (You may have to do this in two batches.) Chill the mixture for 2 hours.

Preheat the oven to 350°F (180°C). Spray 10 straight-sided 6-oz (180-ml) ramekins with cooking spray. Skim off any foam from the top of the chilled mixture, then stir well. Ladle about ⅔ cup (5 oz/140 g) of the mixture into each ramekin. Set the ramekins on a baking sheet and place in the center of the oven.

Bake for 18–20 minutes, rotating once, until puffed. The centers may be a bit loose. Let cool, then run the tip of a sharp knife around the inside to loosen, and chill completely.

Whip the cream until very thick, cover, and chill until firm, at least 4 hours.

To serve, turn the ramekins upside down and gently tap out the *tortas*. Turn each *torta* right side up on a serving plate and top with a generous spoonful of the whipped cream.

COOK'S NOTE: *Crema* (page 177) may be substituted for the heavy cream.

Mexican cooks often use sweet vegetables, like winter squash, as northern cooks would use apples or pears. This lovely *capirotada* includes squash and plump raisins along with vanilla and warm sweet spices. The recipe comes from chef Susana Trilling of Seasons of My Heart Cooking School in Oaxaca.

mexican bread pudding with rum sauce

FOR THE BREAD PUDDING

10 tablespoons (150 g) unsalted butter, melted, plus more for greasing

¾ cup (4½ oz/130 g) raisins

4 cups (1 qt/1 L) whole milk

1½ cups (300 g) sugar

2 tablespoons Grand Marnier

2 teaspoons vanilla extract

1 teaspoon ground cinnamon

1 teaspoon ground nutmeg

⅛ teaspoon fine sea salt

4 large eggs, lightly beaten

1 medium butternut squash, peeled and cut into ½-inch (12-mm) cubes

6 oz (180 g) stale white country bread, cut into 1-inch (2.5-cm) cubes

FOR THE SAUCE

1½ cups (325 g) firmly packed dark brown sugar

8 tablespoons (120 g) butter

½ cup (125 ml) heavy cream

¼ cup (50 ml) rum

⅛ teaspoon fine sea salt

Whipped cream, to serve

serves 8–10

To make the bread pudding, heat the oven to 350°F (180°C). Grease a 9 x 13–inch (23 x 33–cm) glass or ceramic baking dish with a little butter and set aside. Place the raisins in a small bowl and cover with boiling water; let sit for 10 minutes.

Meanwhile, whisk together the melted butter, milk, sugar, Grand Marnier, vanilla, cinnamon, nutmeg, salt, and eggs in a large bowl until smooth. Drain the raisins and stir into the custard mixture along with the squash and bread; let sit for 10 minutes. Pour the mixture into the prepared baking dish and cover with aluminum foil. Bake for 50 minutes, uncover, and continue baking until the bread pudding is golden brown, about 1 hour more.

To make the sauce, bring the brown sugar, butter, heavy cream, rum, and salt to a boil in a 2-qt (2-L) saucepan over medium-high heat, and cook until the sugar dissolves and the sauce thickens slightly, about 5 minutes; set aside and keep warm.

To serve, spoon the bread pudding into serving bowls, drizzle with sauce, and top with a dollop of whipped cream.

COOK'S NOTE: Acorn squash, pumpkin, and even sweet potatoes can be substituted for the butternut squash here.

Rice pudding lovers, this is for you: a creamy-rich concoction that sparkles with fresh lemon, cinnamon, Mexican raw sugar, and the sweetness of dried plums *(ciruelas)*. Be sure to let it set up in the dishes to make the crust. If you don't have a torch to caramelize the top, just sprinkle the crushed *piloncillo* sugar over the top.

rice pudding with dried plums & lemon zest

1 lemon

1 cup (200) medium- or long-grain white rice (not converted)

2-inch (5-cm) stick cinnamon, preferably Mexican *canela,* rinsed in hot water

12 pitted dried plums, quartered

1 cup (250 ml) heavy cream

2¼ cups (525 ml) whole milk

½ vanilla bean or 1 teaspoon vanilla extract

½ cup plus 2 tablespoons (130 g) granulated sugar

4 tablespoons (50 g) raw sugar, preferably Mexican *piloncillo,* crushed to a fine dust

Fresh raspberries, blueberries, or other seasonal fruit

serves 6

With a sharp vegetable peeler, pare 2 lengthwise strips of zest from the lemon, being careful to remove only the yellow zest and not the bitter white pith.

Combine the lemon zest, rice, 2 cups (500 ml) water, the cinnamon stick, and the dried plums in a 2-qt (2-L) saucepan or a double boiler. Bring to a boil and simmer for 5 minutes.

Add the cream, milk, vanilla bean (or extract), and granulated sugar. Bring to a simmer and cook over medium-low heat, stirring often with a wooden spoon until the rice is thoroughly cooked and soft, 20–30 minutes. The rice should be loose and very "saucy." It will thicken as it cools. Remove and discard the cinnamon stick and vanilla bean.

Spoon the pudding into heatproof dishes and chill. To serve, blot the top carefully with a paper towel. Sprinkle about 1 tablespoon *piloncillo* sugar on top and melt with a butane torch before serving with the fruit alongside.

COOK'S NOTE: You can replace the dairy in this recipe with vanilla-flavored soy, almond, or coconut milk.

basic recipes

POT BEANS

2½ cups (18 oz/560 g) dried beans of choice

2 tablespoons safflower or canola oil, lard, or rendered bacon fat

1 white onion, finely chopped

1 clove garlic, minced

1 jalapeño chile, thinly sliced into rings (optional)

2 sprigs fresh epazote, especially if cooking black beans (optional)

Fine sea salt

½ cup (2 oz/60 g) crumbled queso fresco, for serving (optional)

MAKES ABOUT 8 CUPS (1.75 KG);
SERVES 4 AS A MAIN COURSE

Pick over the beans and discard any broken beans or small stones or other debris. Rinse well, place in a large pot, and add water to cover by several inches. Bring to a boil, then reduce the heat until the water is barely simmering.

Meanwhile, in a small frying pan, heat the oil, lard, or bacon fat over medium heat. Add the onion and sauté until dark yellow, about 4 minutes. Stir in the garlic and jalapeño (if using), and cook for 1 minute longer. Add this mixture to the beans, reduce the heat to medium-low, cover partially, and cook until the beans are just tender, about 2 hours. The timing depends on the age of the beans. Stir the beans from time to time and, if necessary, pour in enough hot water to keep the water level at 1 inch (2.5 cm) above the beans.

Add the epazote (if using) and 1 teaspoon salt and continue to cook until the beans are quite soft, about 40 minutes longer. Again, the timing may vary. (If time allows, let the beans cool in the broth. The earthy flavor will intensify if the beans are stored, covered, in the refrigerator for at least overnight, then slowly reheated. They will keep for up to 4 days.)

If serving the beans as they are, ladle the broth and beans into warmed bowls and garnish with the crumbled cheese, if desired.

REFRIED BEANS

These homey *frijoles refritos* are not actually beans that have been fried twice, but soupy pot beans that are coarsely mashed and then fried until dry. For an attractive presentation, it is common to form the beans into a long roll before garnishing them.

½ cup (4 oz/100 g) lard or ½ cup (125 ml) safflower or canola oil, plus more as needed

½ white onion, finely chopped

4 cups (24 oz/680 g) Pot Beans (at left) or other cooked beans, plus 2 cups (500 ml) bean broth (see Cook's Note)

3 avocado leaves (page 182), toasted and finely crumbled (optional)

Fine sea salt

⅔ cup (2½ oz/75 g) crumbled queso fresco or fresh goat cheese, for serving (optional)

Fried tortilla chips or strips, for serving (optional)

6 small romaine lettuce leaves, for serving (optional)

8 radishes, with leaves attached, for serving (optional)

MAKES ABOUT 5 CUPS (1.2 KG); SERVES 4–6

In a large, heavy frying pan, heat the lard or oil over medium heat. Add the onion and sauté, stirring frequently, until soft and golden, about 5 minutes.

Pour in 1 cup (6 oz/180 g) of the beans with 1 cup (250 ml) of the broth, smashing the beans down with the back of a large wooden spoon. Continue until the remaining beans and broth have been mashed to a coarse purée. Stir in the avocado leaves, if using, raise the heat to medium-high, and cook, stirring occasionally, until the purée begins to dry out, 10–15 minutes, adding more lard or oil if needed. Season to taste with salt. If desired, form the beans into a roll: fry them until they draw away from the edges of the pan, and then lift one edge of the pan and tip the solidified mass of beans over on itself.

If serving the beans as they are, transfer to a platter or individual plates and garnish with cheese, if desired. The fried tortilla chips can be stuck in the mound of beans as a decoration and as a way to scoop them up. Add the lettuce leaves and red radishes on the side for color contrast, if you like.

COOK'S NOTE: If using canned beans, rinse, and substitute 1 cup (250 ml) water for the bean broth.

BEEF STOCK

6 lb (3 kg) meaty beef and veal shanks

2 yellow onions, coarsely chopped

1 leek, white and tender green parts, coarsely chopped

2 carrots, coarsely chopped

1 rib celery, coarsely chopped

6 cloves garlic

4 sprigs fresh flat-leaf parsley

3 sprigs fresh thyme

2 small bay leaves

10–12 black peppercorns

MAKES ABOUT 5 QT (5 L)

In a stockpot, combine the beef and veal shanks and add cold water to cover. Place the pot over medium-high heat and slowly bring almost to a boil. Using a large spoon, skim off any scum and froth from the surface. Reduce the heat to low and simmer uncovered, skimming the surface as needed and adding more water if necessary to keep the shanks immersed, for 2 hours.

Add the onions, leek, carrots, celery, garlic, parsley, thyme, bay leaves, and peppercorns and continue to simmer over low heat, uncovered, until the meat begins to fall from the bones and the stock is very flavorful, about 2 hours longer.

Remove from the heat and let stand until the liquid is almost room temperature, about 1 hour. Line a fine-mesh sieve with cheesecloth, set over a heatproof container, and pour the stock through the sieve. Discard the solids. Use a large metal spoon to skim the clear yellow fat from the surface of the stock and use right away. Alternatively, let the stock cool to room temperature, then cover and refrigerate until fully chilled. Using a spoon, lift off the congealed layer of fat on top and discard. Cover and refrigerate for up to 5 days or freeze in airtight containers for up to 2 months.

CHICKEN STOCK

5 lb (2.5 kg) chicken backs and necks

1 leek, white and tender green parts, coarsely chopped

2 carrots, coarsely chopped

1 rib celery, coarsely chopped

12 sprigs fresh flat-leaf parsley

1 sprig fresh thyme

8–10 black peppercorns

MAKES ABOUT 3½ QT (3.5 L)

In a stockpot, combine the chicken parts, leek, carrots, celery, parsley, thyme, and peppercorns. Add cold water to cover by 1 inch (2.5 cm). Place the pot over medium-high heat and slowly bring almost to a boil. Using a large spoon, skim off any foam from the surface. Reduce the heat to low and simmer, uncovered, skimming the surface as needed and adding more water to keep the ingredients immersed, until the meat has fallen off the bones and the stock is fragrant and flavorful, about 3 hours.

Remove from the heat and let stand until the liquid is almost room temperature, about 1 hour. Line a fine-mesh sieve with cheesecloth, set over a heatproof container, and pour the stock through the sieve. Discard the solids. Use a large metal spoon to skim and discard the clear yellow fat from the surface of the stock and use the stock right away. Alternatively, let the stock cool to room temperature, then cover and refrigerate until fully chilled. Using a spoon, lift off the congealed layer of fat on top and discard. Cover and refrigerate for up to 5 days or freeze in airtight containers for up to 2 months.

VEGETABLE STOCK

4–5 peppercorns

4 sprigs fresh flat-leaf parsley

1 sprig fresh thyme

1 bay leaf

¼ cup (60 ml) olive oil

1 yellow onion, coarsely chopped

1 carrot, peeled and coarsely chopped

2 ribs celery, coarsely chopped

½ cup (125 ml) dry white wine

MAKES ABOUT 3 QT (3 L)

Wrap the peppercorns, parsley, thyme, and bay leaf in cheesecloth and secure with kitchen string.

In a stockpot over medium heat, warm the oil until shimmering. Add the onion, carrot, and celery and sauté until lightly browned, 5–8 minutes. Add the wine and deglaze the pot, stirring to scrape up the browned bits from the pan bottom. Raise the heat to medium-high and cook until the wine is almost completely evaporated. Add 4 qt (4 L) water and the herb bundle and bring to a boil. Reduce the heat to low and let simmer, uncovered, for about 45 minutes.

Strain the stock through a sieve into a heatproof container and discard the solids. Let the stock cool completely, stirring it occasionally to help the heat dissipate. Cover and refrigerate for up to 2 days or freeze in airtight containers for up to 3 months.

TOMATILLO SAUCE

12 tomatillos

2 cloves garlic

½ small onion

2 jalapeño chiles, seeded

¼ cup (7 g) chopped cilantro

MAKES 3 CUPS (700 ML)

Bring a large pot of water to a boil over high heat. Husk and rinse the tomatillos. Reduce the heat to medium-high, add the tomatillos, and cook until they soften and become paler in color, 3–4 minutes.

Transfer the tomatillos to a colander and let cool. Roughly chop all the ingredients and combine in a blender or food processor, and purée. Use right away as directed in a recipe, or store in an airtight container in the refrigerator for up to 5 days. This sauce will also keep in the freezer for several months; purée in a blender after thawing.

RED CHILE SAUCE

10 large dried guajillo or ancho chiles

1 plum tomato, chopped

4 cloves garlic

Fine sea salt

2 teaspoons vegetable oil

3 tablespoons finely minced white onion

MAKES 4 CUPS (1 QT/1 L)

Heat a large, heavy frying pan or griddle over medium-high heat. Wipe the chiles clean with a dry paper towel. Working in batches, place the chiles in the hot pan and press with a spatula, holding them flat for about 10 seconds each. Turn the chiles and press flat on the other side for 20–30 seconds longer, being careful not to let them burn. Transfer the chiles to a plate and let cool. When cool enough to handle, remove the stems, seeds, and ribs and tear the chiles into pieces. Transfer to a bowl, pour in 2 cups (500 ml) water, and stir well. Let soak at room temperature, stirring several times, until well softened, about 1 hour.

Transfer the chiles and their soaking liquid to a blender. Add the tomato, garlic, and 1 teaspoon salt and process to a thick, smooth purée.

In a frying pan, heat the oil over medium heat. Add the onion and cook, stirring often, until just softened, 3–5 minutes. Pour the chile purée into the frying pan. Add ¼ cup (50 ml) water to the unrinsed blender, swirl to wash down the residue of the purée from the sides, and add to the pan. Fry the sauce, stirring constantly, until fragrant and slightly thickened, 3–5 minutes.

Add enough water to make 4 cups (1 qt/1 L) sauce, or thin to the desired consistency. (The sauce will thicken when fried with tortillas for chilaquiles, page 70.) Taste and adjust the seasoning, if needed. Serve right away, or store in an airtight container in the refrigerator for up to 5 days. This sauce will also keep in the freezer for several months; purée in a blender after thawing.

SEASONED WHITE RICE

2 cups (14 oz/440 g) medium- or long-grain white rice

½ white onion, coarsely chopped

2 cloves garlic

5 tablespoons (75 ml) canola oil

½ teaspoon fresh lime juice

3 sprigs fresh flat-leaf parsley

Fine sea salt

SERVES 6

Rinse the rice in water, swishing the grains, and then drain. Repeat two or three times, draining well. Spread the rice out on a kitchen towel and let stand to air-dry for about 10 minutes.

Put the onion, garlic, and 3 tablespoons cold water in a blender and process until smooth.

In a Dutch oven, warm the oil over medium-high heat until it is smoking. Add the rice and cook, stirring, until the rice has absorbed the oil and the grains turn a toasty golden color, have a nutty aroma, and begin to crackle, 7–10 minutes.

Stir the onion purée into the rice and cook, stirring, for 1 minute. Pour in 4 cups (1 L) hot water and add the lime juice, parsley, and 1 teaspoon salt. Bring to a simmer, then reduce the heat to medium-low, cover, and cook for 15 minutes without lifting the lid.

Remove from the heat and let stand, covered, for 10 minutes. Transfer the rice to individual plates or a serving bowl and discard the parsley sprigs. Fluff the grains gently with a fork and serve hot.

COCONUT RICE

1–3 large green (young) coconut(s)

Canned fresh or frozen coconut water as needed

1 cup (7 oz/220 g) medium- or long-grain white rice

⅓ cup (2 oz/60 g) raisins

1 teaspoon unsalted butter

Fine sea salt

MAKES 4–6 SERVINGS

Place each coconut on its side and, using a cleaver, shave off the top portion of the white husk around the tip to expose a "lid" of shell. Whack the exposed coconut shell to cut it along the seam, rotating the fruit in a circle and continuing to make cuts until the lid is scored completely around the perimeter. Pry

the lid open and pour the coconut water through a fine-mesh sieve placed over a measuring pitcher. Using a metal spoon or ice-cream scoop, scrape the inside of the coconut to remove the meat.

Measure out 2½ cups (625 ml) coconut water. Depending on the size and number of coconuts you are using, add canned fresh or frozen coconut water as needed to equal 2½ cups. Finely chop the coconut meat and measure out ½ cup (60 g). (Reserve the remaining coconut meat and water for another use.)

In a saucepan with a tight-fitting lid, combine the coconut water, rice, raisins, butter, and 1 teaspoon salt. Stir once to settle and bring to a gentle boil over medium heat. Cover and reduce the heat to low. Cook until all of the liquid has been absorbed, 15–20 minutes. Do not stir.

Remove from the heat and let stand, covered, for 5 minutes. Transfer the rice to individual plates or a serving bowl and fluff the grains gently with a fork. Gently stir in the coconut meat and serve hot.

CREMA

1 cup (250 ml) heavy cream (not ultrapasteurized)

1 tablespoon buttermilk or plain yogurt with active cultures

MAKES 1 CUP (250 ML)

In a bowl, mix the cream with the buttermilk. Cover with plastic wrap, poke a few holes in the wrap, and place in a warm spot (85°F/30°C) until thickened and set, 8–24 hours. Stir, cover, and refrigerate until chilled and firm before using or for up to 1 week.

CILANTRO-LIME CREMA: In a small serving bowl, stir together ⅓ cup (2½ oz/70 g) *crema*, 1 tablespoon fresh lime juice, ¼ cup (15 g) minced fresh cilantro, 1 tablespoon minced chipotle chiles in adobo, and a pinch of fine sea salt. Taste and adjust the seasoning. Cover and refrigerate until ready to use.

WORKING WITH FRESH PEPPERS & CHILES

Capsaicin, the compound in chiles that is responsible for their heat level, can cause pain if it comes into contact with eyes or other parts of the body. If possible, wear disposable gloves when handling chiles.

TO ROAST: If using a gas stove, using tongs, hold the peppers or chiles over a high flame and roast, turning often, until the skin is charred and blistered, 2–3 minutes. If using a charcoal or gas grill, place the peppers or chiles on the grill over a very hot fire for 3–5 minutes, turning often with tongs. If using a broiler, set an oven rack 6 inches (15 cm) from the heat source. Place the peppers or chiles on an aluminum foil–lined pan and broil, turning often, until blackened, 5–10 minutes. (Broiled peppers and chiles will be too soft to stuff but can be used for other recipes.)

TO REMOVE THE SKIN: After roasting, place the peppers or chiles in a paper bag or heatproof bowl covered with plastic wrap and let sweat for about 8 minutes to loosen the skin. This will also soften the flesh, so do not leave them too long. Pick and peel away as much skin as possible. Don't worry if some charred bits remain.

TO SEED: If stuffing the pepper or chile, use a small knife to cut a lengthwise slit in each chile from the stem end to the bottom, leaving ½ inch (12 mm) uncut on top and at least ¼ inch (6 mm) on the bottom. Leaving the stem intact, remove the seeds and membranes with a small spoon and/or your fingers. Wipe the inside with a damp towel and dry well. For slicing or chopping, cut a lengthwise slit and spread it flat on a cutting surface. Cut out the stem, then scrape away the seeds and membranes with your fingers and a knife.

WORKING WITH DRIED CHILES

TO SEED: Clean the chiles with a damp cloth. Split them lengthwise, then use a small, sharp knife to remove the seeds.

TO TOAST: Clean the chiles with a damp cloth. Heat a heavy frying pan over medium heat. Add the whole or seeded chiles to the pan. Press down firmly for several seconds with a spatula, then turn the chiles and press down for a few seconds more before removing. The chiles should change color only slightly and start to give off their aroma.

TO CRUSH OR GRIND: Stem the chiles and seed, if desired. Tear the chiles into small pieces. To crush, add the pieces to a mortar and use a pestle to break up into smaller pieces. To grind, add the chile pieces to a spice grinder or a clean coffee grinder. Grind until the chiles form a fine powder.

PAN-ROASTING VEGETABLES

To pan-roast vegetables and aromatics such as tomatoes, husked tomatillos, onions, and garlic, place an aluminum foil–lined heavy frying pan over medium-high heat. Place the vegetables on the foil and roast until the flesh is soft and the skins are blackened on all sides. Let the vegetables sit undisturbed as they blacken, turning just a few times to roast all sides. The garlic and chiles will be done first, in about 5 minutes; the tomatoes and tomatillos will take 10–15 minutes. The blackened skin of the tomatoes and tomatillos and the skin of the garlic and onions, if remaining, is often removed before using.

USING A TORTILLA PRESS

Line a tortilla press with 2 sheets of plastic wrap. Or, cut a quart-sized plastic storage bag along the sides, leaving the bottom seam of the bag intact. Place the opened up storage bag in the tortilla press.

Place a dough ball between the plastic and gently push down the top plate of the press. You might need to rotate the dough once or twice and press again to produce the desired shape. Open the press and peel off the top sheet of plastic. Invert the tortilla onto one hand and remove the remaining plastic.

STERILIZING JARS

A simple method of sterilizing a jar for pickles is to wash it in hot soapy water, then run it through the dishwasher on a hot rinse cycle. Alternatively, boil the jar for 10 minutes in a large saucepan of water, then place on a baking sheet in a 300°F (150°C) oven to dry.

drinks

GREEN GRAPE & MELON COOLER

2 lb (1 kg) seedless green grapes

1 very ripe honeydew melon, halved, seeded, peeled, and cut into chunks

Juice of 1 lime

¼–½ cup (50–100 g) sugar

2 cups (500 ml) cold sparkling water

2 limes, quartered, or honeydew slivers for garnish

SERVES 8

In a blender, combine half the grapes, half the melon, and half the lime juice with 1 cup (250 ml) still water. Purée until smooth and pour into a bowl. Add the remaining grapes, melon, lime juice, and 1 cup (250 ml) more still water to the blender and purée until smooth. Add to the bowl. Add sugar to taste and mix well.

Pour the fruit mixture through a medium-mesh sieve into a pitcher. Add the sparkling water. Serve in tall glasses over ice, garnished with a lime wedge or honeydew sliver.

HIBISCUS AGUA FRESCA

2 cups (6 oz/180 g) dried *jamaica* (hibiscus) flowers (see Cook's Note)

Zest of 1 orange

½ cup (100 g) sugar or ½ cup (170 g) honey

2 tablespoons fresh lime juice

Still water, sparkling water, or fresh orange juice

Lime slices

SERVES 10–12

In a saucepan over medium-high heat, combine 6 cups (1½ qt/1.5 L) water, the *jamaica* flowers, and the orange zest. Bring to a simmer and cook for 5 minutes. Pour into a heatproof glass bowl, stir in the sugar, and let cool for 10 minutes.

Strain the mixture through a fine-mesh sieve into a glass or plastic container and add the lime juice. Taste and add more sugar if necessary. Cover and refrigerate until cold, at least 1 hour or up to 3 days.

To serve, dilute the *agua fresca* to taste with still water, sparkling water, or orange juice. Serve in tall glasses over ice, garnished with the lime slices.

COOK'S NOTE: *Jamaica* flowers are sold packaged as a tea or as a diuretic at health food stores, well-stocked markets, and Latin groceries.

STRAWBERRY AGUA FRESCA

5 cups (750 g) hulled strawberries, plus diced strawberry for garnish

½ cup (100 g) sugar

⅓ cup (75 ml) lime juice

Coarse sea salt

4 sprigs mint (optional)

SERVES 4

Combine half of the strawberries and 1½ cups (350 ml) water in a blender. Purée until smooth. Place a fine-mesh sieve over a bowl. Pour the purée into the sieve, using a silicone spatula to press the mixture through the sieve. Discard the strawberry seeds left in the sieve. Repeat with the remaining strawberries and 1½ cups (350 ml) more water.

Pour the strawberry purée into a pitcher. Stir in the sugar, lime juice, and ¼ teaspoon salt. Add an additional 1–2 cups (250–500 ml) water to reach the desired consistency.

Serve in tall glasses over ice, garnished with diced strawberry and a mint sprig if desired.

WATERMELON AGUA FRESCA

8 cups (3 lb/1.5 kg) peeled, seeded, and cubed watermelon

Fresh lime juice

¼ cup (50 g) sugar

2 cups (500 ml) still or sparkling water

SERVES 10

Place half of the watermelon in a food processor and blend until smooth. Add lime juice to taste and half of the sugar and mix well. Refrigerate until well chilled. Pour the purée into a large pitcher. Repeat with the remaining watermelon, lime juice, and sugar and add to the pitcher. Stir well and add water to thin to the desired consistency. Taste and adjust the flavor with more sugar or lime juice if needed. Serve in tall glasses over ice.

mexican pantry staples

ACHIOTE PASTE This seasoning paste is made from the hard, brick-red seeds of the tropical annatto tree. The seeds are ground with spices and mixed with garlic and vinegar or the juice of bitter oranges. The paste is popular in the Yucatán peninsula, where it lends a mild flowery flavor and deep yellow-orange color to dishes.

ADOBO In Mexico, adobo is a seasoning made from dried chiles, herbs, salt, and spices, ground together with vinegar to the consistency of a thick paste. It is similar to the Spanish mixture of the same name, which calls for vinegar, olive oil, and spices. Because vinegar and salt are natural preservatives, the use of adobo was originally a technique for pickling and preserving meats. Canned chipotle chiles in adobo are widely available and present an easy way to bring delicious smoky flavor to a dish.

AVOCADO LEAVES The leathery leaves of the avocado tree are used as a seasoning in south-central Mexico. They may be used fresh or dried and added whole or crumbled to contribute an aniselike taste to savory dishes.

BANANA LEAVES The large, pliable leaves of the banana tree are used to wrap tamales for steaming and seafood, poultry, or meat for steaming, grilling, or roasting. They protect the food while contributing a mild grassy flavor. Find frozen banana leaves in the freezer section of specialty Latin and Asian markets. Before using the leaves, soften them by steaming them or passing them over a flame.

BEANS A staple of Latin American cuisine, bean varieties come in a virtual kaleidoscope of earthy colors. Most are sold dried, and may require soaking; buy dried beans from a store with high turnover so that they are as fresh as possible and require less cooking time.

Black Also called turtle, Mexican, or Spanish black beans, these small and shiny black beans are used widely for pot beans, soups, and dips.

Black-Eyed Peas Also called cowpeas, field peas, or black-eyed beans, these cream-colored, kidney-shaped beans have a characteristic black dot with a yellow center and a mild flavor. These legumes require less soaking than most dried beans.

Fava Also called broad beans, these large, flat beans are pale green when eaten fresh. The dried version is darker and may be sold with or without its seed coat still intact; be sure to choose the correct one called for in a recipe.

Pinto A pale brown bean with an earthy flavor and darker, sometimes pinkish streaks, which disappear during cooking. This bean is a staple in Mexican refried beans (see page 172).

CHEESE Mexican cuisine is known best for its fresh cheeses, but there are some aged varieties as well.

Cotija This hard, salty, strongly flavored cheese is named after a town in Mexico where it comes from. Its flavor is similar to Parmesan or feta; it is also called queso blanco.

Farmer's Cheese This is a mild form of cottage cheese drained of most liquid. It is sold in a fairly solid loaf shape and is mild and slightly tangy.

Queso Añejo Queso fresco is pressed in a mold to increase density and aged to create queso añejo. The aging process gives the cheese a saltier flavor and a medium sharpness. Like queso fresco, queso añejo is a fine melting cheese; longer aging produces a firmness suitable for grating, so añejo cheese is often used to make an even cheese layer in dishes like enchiladas.

Queso Fresco This fresh, moist, lightly salted cheese is somewhere between ricotta and mild feta in taste and consistency. It may be used for melting.

Queso Menonita This mild, Cheddar-like cheese with an excellent melting quality is made by Mennonite communities in Mexico and Central America.

Queso Oaxaca The state of Oaxaca, Mexico, is famous for its white, string-like cheese, rolled up like giant balls of yarn and stacked in the markets. Like mozzarella, it is the product of a stretching process and is delicious melted.

CHILE CON LIMON This favorite seasoning mix, available ready-made at Latin groceries and well-stocked supermarkets, is a blend of ground chiles, salt, and citrus flavors. It's especially delicious on fresh fruit.

CHILES Whether fresh or dried, chiles have distinctive flavors and degrees of heat, so they typically cannot be used interchangeably.

Anaheim This long, green, and mild to moderately spicy chile is found in most markets; it is similar to the New Mexican variety of chile. In dried form, it is called a California chile.

Ancho The ancho is a dried poblano. It measures 4–5 inches (10–12 cm) long, and has wide shoulders, wrinkled, deep reddish brown skin, and a mild, bittersweet flavor reminiscent of chocolate.

Árbol This smooth-skinned, bright reddish-orange chile, usually found dried, measures about 3 inches (7½ cm) long, is narrow in shape, and tastes fiery hot.

California *See* Anaheim.

Chipotle The smoke-dried form of the ripened jalapeño, this chile is rich in flavor and very hot. It is typically a leathery brown, although some varieties are a deep burgundy.

Guajillo Moderately hot, this burgundy dried chile is about 5 inches (13 cm) long, tapered, and with rather brittle smooth skin and a sharp, uncomplicated flavor.

Güero Also called a banana pepper, this pale yellow, broad-shouldered fresh chile 3–5 inches (7–12 cm) in length varies in heat; some are hotter than a jalapeño, others milder.

Habanero Renowned as the hottest of all chiles, this 2-inch (5-cm) lantern-shaped variety from Yucatán combines its intense heat with flavors of tomatoes and tropical fruits. Available in unripe green and ripened yellow, orange, and red forms, and in fresh and dried forms.

Jalapeño The most popular and widely available of fresh chiles, this tapered chile, 2–3 inches (5–7½ cm) in length, has thick flesh and varies in degree of hotness. It is found in green and sweeter ripened red forms.

Pasilla This skinny, wrinkled, raisin-black dried chile is about 6 inches (15 cm) long, with a sharp, fairly hot flavor.

Poblano Named for the state of Puebla in Mexico, this fresh, broad-shouldered, tapered, moderately hot chile is 5 inches (13 cm) long and a polished deep green.

Serrano These slender chiles measure 1–2 inches (2½–5 cm) long and are very hot, with a brightly acidic flavor; available in both green and ripened red forms.

CHIMICHURRI Borrowed from Argentina, where the condiment is ubiquitous, chimichurri accompanies nearly anything that is fried, grilled, or roasted and may also be used as a marinade. The texture ranges from smooth to chunky, and the ingredients vary, but the constants are olive oil, vinegar or lemon juice, garlic, and herbs.

CHOCOLATE Cocoa beans are native to the tropics and were a major culinary contribution of the New World. Today, so-called Mexican chocolate is sold in large tablets and contains ground cacao, sugar, cinnamon, and sometimes almonds. Blended with milk it makes *champurrada*, or Mexican hot chocolate. Chocolate also marries with spices in the famous mole sauce (page 87).

CHORIZO Mexican chorizo is ground pork heavily seasoned with chile and garlic, stuffed into casings, and hung for several days to allow the flavors to mellow before using. Unlike the milder, dry-cured Spanish chorizo, this sausage must be cooked. It can be purchased freshly made at Mexican markets and at many butcher shops. Never purchase chorizo prepackaged in plastic, or your dish will be greasy and disappointing in flavor. Spanish chorizo may be substituted, but add additional ground chile to the sausage once it is removed from its casings, or use hot Italian sausage.

COCONUT Grown on palm trees in tropical climates, the coconut is the world's largest nut. Its nutmeat is firm, creamy, and snowy white, and is a favorite ingredient for sweet baked goods. When selecting a fresh coconut, shake it to be sure it's full of coconut water, and pass up any with signs of mold around the "eyes." For more on working with fresh coconut, see Coconut Rice, page 177.

COCONUT MILK Coconut milk differs from coconut water. The milk is extracted from grated coconut meat. Canned unsweetened coconut milk, available in full-fat and reduced-fat forms, is a fine convenience product. Don't confuse this with sweetened coconut mixes for mixed drinks, or products labeled coconut cream or coconut water.

COCONUT, SHREDDED Bags of shredded dried coconut are available in the baking supply aisles

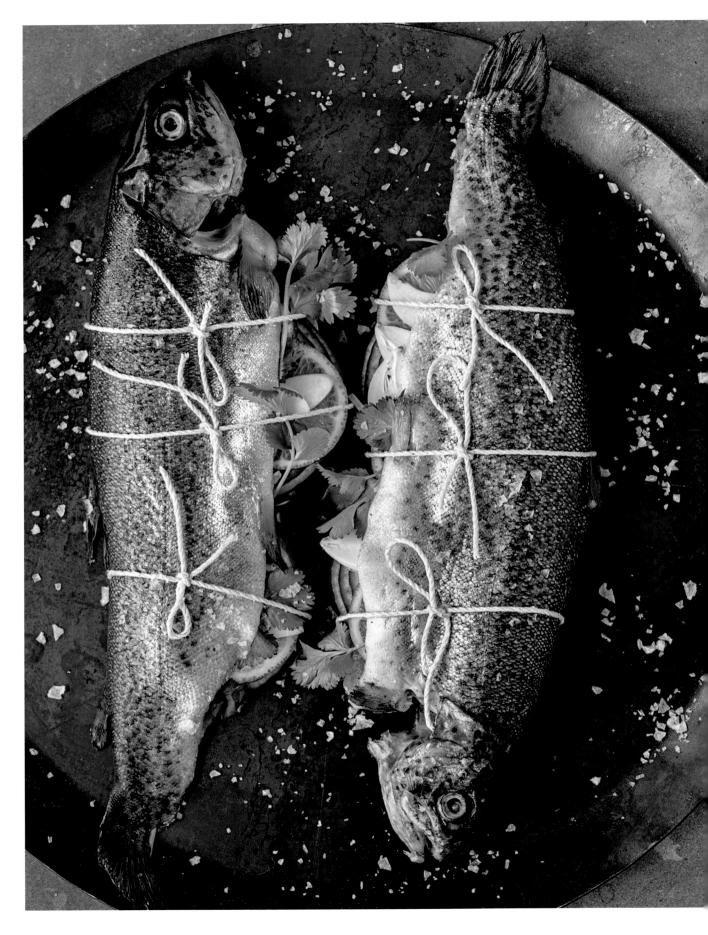

of most supermarkets. Shredded dried coconut is almost always sweetened, but it is possible to buy it unsweetened. Check the bag and your recipe to make sure you have the correct type.

EGGS, RAW Uncooked eggs carry a risk of being infected with salmonella or other bacteria, which can lead to food poisoning. This risk is of most concern to young children, older people, pregnant women, and anyone with a compromised immune system. If you have health and safety concerns, do not consume raw egg; rather, seek out a pasteurized egg product to replace it. Eggs can be made safe by heating them to 160°F (71°C).

EPAZOTE Considered a tenacious weed by many gardeners, pungent epazote (also called wormseed) is looked on as a culinary treasure by Mexican cooks. Ideally, epazote is used fresh, but dried epazote, stocked in Mexican markets, can be used in beans and soups. Enclose about 1 teaspoon in a tea ball for easy removal of the woody stems.

FLAN Originally introduced to the New World by Spain, this decadent dessert is beloved in Mexico and throughout Latin America. Rich with eggs and cream or sweetened condensed milk, flan is baked in caramel-lined ramekins, which are chilled then inverted before serving, creating an irresistible caramel topping for the custard.

HEART OF PALM The tender, edible core of a young cabbage palm tree is a delicacy in tropical countries. Hearts of palm are slender and white, with many thin, concentric layers, like a leek. They resemble white asparagus, and taste similar to artichokes. They may be served as part of a salad, or included in lightly cooked dishes. Fresh hearts of palm are rare, but they are commonly available canned in water.

HIBISCUS Used to make *agua de jamaica,* the dried red calyxes that surround the yellow petals of the *Hibiscus sabdariffa* (a smaller version of the showier ornamental) are sold packaged as a tea or as a diuretic in health food stores, well-stocked markets, and in Latin grocery stores.

JICAMA A member of the large legume family, the crunchy, ivory-fleshed, brown-skinned jicama is a tuber used throughout Mexico, its country of origin. Jicama has a bland taste that benefits from being marinated raw in lime juice or from being combined with fruits or vegetables. Before using, peel away the skin and the fibrous layer beneath it with a sharp knife.

JAMAICA *See* Hibiscus.

KAHLÚA This brand-name coffee liqueur is similar to *crème de cacao* and is also a frequent ingredient in desserts. Other good-quality coffee liqueurs may be substituted. It pairs particularly well with milk or cream, as in the popular White Russian cocktail.

MANGO Native to India, but grown in tropical climates worldwide, this fragrant, oval-shaped fruit has skin that ranges from green to pale yellow or orange. The flesh is sweet, juicy, and aromatic. Ripe mangoes give slightly when pressed and are highly fragrant at their stem end. To cut a mango, use the tip of your knife to locate the wide, flat pit, and start by cutting the flesh away from the flat sides, or cheeks. You can either peel the mango before cutting, or cut the flesh away with the skin still attached, then slice or dice as you would avocado flesh, and lastly invert the skin and slice the flesh away from the peel.

MASA AND MASA HARINA Masa, the dough used for making tortillas, tamales, and many snacks such as quesadillas and sopes, is the foundation of much of Mexican cooking. It is made by boiling dried corn kernels with slaked lime to remove their tough skins, and then grinding them to form the dough. When possible, use freshly ground masa from a local tortilla factory or other source—there is nothing like it. Masa can also be made from packaged masa harina, which is ground dried masa, but it will not have the same body or flavor as the freshly made dough. Maseca brand is a good choice.

MOLE These traditional complex sauce preparations are often reserved for special celebrations in Mexico. There are many types of moles that span a full spectrum of colors and flavors: *amarillo* (yellow), *verde* (green), *manchamateles* ("stains tablecloths"). The iconic *mole poblano* is nearly black in color, infused with spices and chocolate.

NOPALES The paddles of the cactus plant, nopales are widely used in a variety of preparations in Mexico. They are often sliced or chopped and added to soups, stews, and salads, or stirred in with rice, beans, and eggs. The cactus becomes slimy when boiled, so it's important to rinse it under running cold water as soon as it is tender. You can also add a little baking soda or a copper coin to the pot while the cactus cooks to reduce the slimy effect.

ORANGE, BITTER Also known as the Seville orange or sour orange and native to southeast Asia, the bitter orange was the first orange to arrive in the New World by way of Spain. It has a thick peel and bitter juice. It is often used to make marmalades and acidic sauce, such as *pibil* sauce.

OREGANO, MEXICAN A member of the mint family, oregano is an aromatic, pungent, and spicy herb, used as a seasoning for all kinds of savory dishes. It is common in the Mediterranean, but the Mexican variety is much stronger and spicier in flavor. Both varieties of oregano are widely available.

PAPAYA With its distinctive earthy aroma and flavor, papaya is the quintessential tropical fruit. Native to Central America, the fruit looks like a large pear, with thin, pale green skin with blotches of yellow and orange. It's hollow center holds a mass of small, slick black seeds, which are edible and have a slightly peppery flavor. The Mexican variety of papaya is larger than the Hawaiian-grown one, with a rosy flesh and less-sweet flavor.

PICO DE GALLO Also known as *salsa mexicana* or *salsa crudo, pico de gallo* is a chunky fresh Mexican salsa. The salsa is made with a combination of ripe tomatoes, finely chopped white onion, chopped fresh cilantro (fresh coriander), and chiles, such as serrano or jalapeño, are simply tossed with a little lime juice and salt.

PILONCILLO This unrefined sugar is an everyday sweetener, mainly produced in Colombia. Dark brown boiled sugarcane syrup is hardened in cone-, bar-, or disk-shaped molds. The molds can be quite hard and often need to be chopped into pieces, though they will dissolve easily in liquid. Dark brown sugar can be substituted.

PLANTAINS Closely related to the banana, the plantain is larger, starchier, and firmer. When ripe, fresh plantains have almost uniformly black skins and will yield to gentle pressure. It must always be cooked before eating, but unlike the banana, the sturdy plantain won't fall apart or become mushy when baked, stewed, panfried, or deep-fried.

PUMPKIN SEEDS Called *pepitas* in Spanish, pumpkin seeds have been used by Mexican cooks since pre-Columbian times. Whether fat or skinny, raw or roasted, hulled or not, tasty pepitas are an essential ingredient in many sweets, snacks, and savory dishes. Raw green pumpkin seeds can be found in natural-foods stores and in many supermarkets. Toasting makes the hulls crisp and edible.

SAFFRON The orange-red stamens of a crocus flower, saffron is among the most treasured spices in the world. The distinctive earthy flavor and rich gold color make it worth its high price. Threads are sold in small quantities; store them in a cool, dark place, and crush before using. Saffron lends its characteristic vibrant yellow tint to both paella-style rice dishes (page 67) and the beloved *arroz con pollo* (page 65).

SALSA Literally translated, salsa means "sauce," and may refer to any sauce made with a wide range of ingredients, from chiles to chocolate. Non-Spanish speakers, however, think of the quintessential chile-fruit-cilantro combinations, either cooked or raw.

SQUID Caught off the coasts of Mexico, this soft-bodied shellfish has a mild, sweet flavor and a slightly chewy texture that is at its best when quickly cooked or slowly simmered. Fresh squid has a mild, delicate taste and a light gray color. *Chipirones* are baby squid; they are especially tender and sweet.

TEQUILA This liquor is made from the distilled juice of the blue agave plant. *Blanco* (silver or white) tequila may go directly from the still to the bottle, but is often left to settle first for a few weeks in steel vats. Caramel coloring is added to *blanco* to create gold tequila. *Reposado* tequila must spend 2 to 12 weeks in wooden casks, while the more refined *añejo* spends at least a year in wood and often longer.

TOMATILLO Like the tomato, the tomatillo is a member of the nightshade family. It is covered with a parchment-like husk, which is removed. The fruits, which have a unique texture and tart flavor, are the basis for many cooked sauces and moles, and are occasionally used raw in salsas. Carefully rinse off the sticky residue that covers the skin before using.

index

weldon**owen**

Weldon Owen is a division of Bonnier Publishing USA
1045 Sansome Street, Suite 100, San Francisco, CA 94111
www.weldonowen.com

WELDON OWEN, INC.

President & Publisher Roger Shaw
SVP, Sales & Marketing Amy Kaneko

Associate Publisher Amy Marr
Project Editor Sarah Putman Clegg

Creative Director Kelly Booth
Art Director Marisa Kwek
Senior Production Designer Rachel Lopez Metzger

Production Director Chris Hemesath
Associate Production Director Michelle Duggan

Imaging Manager Don Hill

Photographer John Lee
Food Stylist Lillian Kang
Prop Stylist Glenn Jenkins

Rustic Mexican

Conceived and produced by Weldon Owen, Inc.
In collaboration with Williams Sonoma, Inc.
3250 Van Ness Avenue, San Francisco, CA 94109

A WELDON OWEN PRODUCTION

Library of Congress Cataloging-in-Publication
data is available.

ISBN: 978-1-68188-266-6

Printed and bound in China by 1010 Printing, Ltd.

First printed in 2017
10 9 8 7 6 5 4 3 2 1

ACKNOWLEDGMENTS

Weldon Owen wishes to thank the following people for their generous support
in producing this book: Lesley Bruynesteyn, Gloria Geller, Veronica Laramie,
Elizabeth Parsons, and Molly Stetson.